A. E. King
7 Jan 1988

T·H·E
BEGINNING
O·F
FOREVER

SHIRLEY SEALY

Deseret Book Company
Salt Lake City, Utah

First printing November 1987

Library of Congress Cataloging-in-Publication Data

Sealy, Shirley.
    The beginning of forever.

    1. Maxfield, Judy Sealy, d. 1986—Health.
2. Leukemia—Patients—Utah—Biography.   3. Sealy,
Shirley.   4. Mothers—Utah—Biography.   5. Christian
life—Mormon authors.   I. Title.
RC643.M39S43   1987   362.1'96189299'419 [B]   87-24467
ISBN 0-87579-113-1

To Judy, with love

PREFACE

This is a true love story. It is a story about daily decision making in a family and about my daughter Judy's fight for life. The story is built on the love, support, obedience, and dedication of all those involved—to each other and to the will and blessings of Heavenly Father. It is about personal testimonies of faith and the sure knowledge that our Father in heaven loves us, whatever our problem, much more than we have the knowledge or ability to love each other.

I tried very hard not to write this book. I didn't want to watch Judy go through so much and then to write it all down. But her life, her many friends, those who wrote and said she had changed their lives . . . there was so much. The thoughts wouldn't go away, wouldn't leave me alone. We, as a family, feel very private about our lives, but Judy's story is a missionary message. We couldn't let it end in her grave. Hers is a story that will live on to influence the lives of others now that she is gone, as it did while she lived.

This is my effort to ensure that Judy's missionary work and inspirational life will go on and will continue to help others face what they have to face, will give them courage, and will let them know she had a strong testimony of Jesus Christ and was wise enough to let that testimony guide her to trust her Heavenly Father with her life.

She taught me how to live and she taught me how to die.

CHAPTER 1

"Come Mother, come . . . I'm in so much pain. Neal is taking me to the doctor. Will you come and be with the children?"

"I'll leave right now, Judy."

Hanging up the telephone, I grabbed a small overnight bag and threw in a change of clothes, a toothbrush, and a nightgown. *Just in case*, I said to myself as I picked up my purse and keys and ran for the car.

Judy was in trouble. I had been worried about her even before I went to Atlanta for Christmas. She looked tired and she had been ill.

Her father, Milton, and I were away only a week, but I was startled when I saw her. We had arrived home on Wednesday, New Year's day, and she and her husband, Neal, had stopped by that Saturday.

"You're so skinny!" I'd said as I hugged her.

"I know," she answered with a smile. "That's the only good part about this—I'm down to my ideal size."

"But you're ill. Your color isn't good."

"I know. I've been having some tests."

"What have they found?"

"Well, I asked the doctor if I had cancer and he said he didn't find any. I'm anemic and I have two kidney stones. One is very large. The doctor said it's probably been there about a year, causing a low-grade infection, which could be why I'm anemic."

"What are you going to do about that?"

"I'll probably have to have it out. I could wait until we go to the candy convention in Phoenix and have it removed by ultrasound. They haven't got a machine like that here."

We'd talked a while and then they had left, but I couldn't get Judy off my mind. There was a frailness about her that stayed with me. I found myself praying about her several times a day. Then the call . . .

Judy didn't ask for help very often. She had always prided herself on being independent and was always more involved with helping others than with asking for help herself. The call, even more than the sound of her voice, moved me to action. I knew this was serious.

As I drove to Salt Lake City, forty-five minutes away, my mind went back over events of the last few months. In November, just before Thanksgiving, she had looked radiant and lovely.

"A teenager again," I'd said. "Are you overdoing, as usual, or eating less?"

"About the same. I've been sick. I guess that's why I get so exhausted at night."

Judy was the one who enjoyed sports and exercise along with teaching dancing, and she felt that these activities kept her fit for her busy schedule.

"Judy, you need some time to get well."

"I know. As soon as Christmas and my dance concert are over and I finish decorating my house, I'm going to take time to be sick."

"Can I help?"

"I'll be all right."

"You'll let me know?"

"Yes, if I can't handle it."

But she didn't let me know. And I'd worried, even to the point of calling Neal at work to tell him I felt that she was ill, and to ask him if he'd let me know what I could do to help. He had thanked me and said he was going to help her paint the bathroom that night.

The road curved and I swung onto the freeway cutoff that took me to Judy's home. I pulled into the driveway just as Judy and Neal were getting into their car.

"What is it?" I asked as she kissed me.

"I think it's my kidney stone."

"Oh, Judy, no wonder you're in so much pain!" She nodded and got into the car beside Neal. Through the window she gave me a few instructions about her children, and then they drove away.

Inside the house, Judy's youngest son, four-year-old Derek, ran to me and I hugged him. Derek, who was dark and had sparkling eyes, spent a lot of time with Judy, and I knew he would miss her and wouldn't understand if she had to go to the hospital. I hoped it wouldn't come to that.

"Will you play with me while your mother's gone?" I asked as I followed him to his room, where he had his toys.

"Yes, but she's my 'sweety pie,' " he said. "Is she coming back soon?"

"The doctor's going to find out what makes her hurt."

"And fix it?"

"Of course," I said, and he seemed satisfied.

Neal and Judy had five children. Tucker, thirteen years old, was the eldest. He was a natural actor and enjoyed sports and Scouting. He had stayed with me sometimes when he was little, but since then I hadn't had him around much except at Bear Lake in the summers.

The second child, Maren, who was eleven, was a dancer, like her mother, and a member of a girls' drill team. She also water skiied like her mother.

Then came Spencer, who was ten. He was a neat dresser, had a unique way of doing things, and liked to do everything himself. Spencer had grown up wearing a costume for every character he wanted to be, and he changed with the current TV programs.

Next came Lyndsy, age seven. She was a little Judy. It was fun to watch Judy trying to keep up with Lyndsy. Now she knew how I had felt when *she* was little.

While Derek played in his room, I looked around the house at the redecorating projects Judy and Neal had started before Christmas and which were almost finished. Tucker and Maren were each getting their own rooms, the nursery was being redecorated for Lyndsy, and Spencer and Derek would share a room.

I walked into Lyndsy's room, which was shiny with new paint. The carpet had been removed, and rolls of wallpaper lay on the floor, still packaged, beside Judy's paint-speckled shoes. She had been painting when the pain started.

I picked up a razor blade and started scraping the dried paint off the windows. It was easier not to worry if I kept busy, and I could see plenty of things to do. I decided this would be a good time to help Judy without her asking. Maybe I could help her catch up so she could rest when she came home. She would need rest to get over a kidney-stone operation—I supposed that would be the result of her doctor's visit. A kidney-stone operation usually wasn't complicated, with the new methods available. But any operation was always a concern.

It was some comfort for me, as her mother, to know there was something I could do that might help. And while I worked, my thoughts were about Judy—wonderful, energetic Judy.

Milt and I had five children, and Judy was number two. Even as a child, she had a way of making us all move faster. She also had a tender heart, though she was outspoken and didn't have time for sentiment.

One year when she was just little, her big sister, Vicki, had made a Mother's Day present in school for me. When she gave me her gift, I kissed her and made a fuss about her thoughtfulness. Judy didn't even seem to notice. But that night, as I put Judy to bed, she put her arms around me, hugged me tight, and said, "When I get big I am going to buy you the most wonderful present in the whole world." She was more sensitive than I realized. She was also our active one. As I worked, I remembered how quiet the house was whenever she was away, and how loud we all became when she returned.

I hoped Judy wasn't going to be ill very long. Not that she didn't know what pain and sickness meant. As a child, she had had Perthes' disease, a softening of the hip bone, and had spent eighteen months on crutches, with her leg tied up in a sling. She still carried the limp of that childhood disease.

A quick, detailed memory came as I thought about Judy and her crutches. She had thought her crutches made her popular, and I guess they had, in a way. But the things I learned from that period of her life went much deeper than popularity. It was the first time I had learned to fast and pray meaningfully and to put myself and my family in the hands of the Lord. It was all connected with Judy and school.

Vicki, Judy's older sister, was her best friend. They were three and a half years apart in age. Vicki had waited for her baby sister with excitement, but she had been disappointed when Judy wouldn't lie quietly and let her mother her. In time Judy felt more secure in Vicki's arms, and soon she followed Vicki everywhere, doing just what Vicki did.

There weren't any children Judy's age in our neighborhood, so when Vicki went to school, Judy was lonely. All she could talk about was going to school. There was no kindergarten in our area, so it was a long wait.

The day she and I stood in line to register her for first grade, two women standing beside us with their little girls made quite a fuss over Judy's bright red hair and how pretty she looked in her new green dress. The other little girls didn't like that, and they started whispering to each other, giggling and pointing at Judy. The next day at school it was even worse; they pushed her down and wouldn't play with her.

A few weeks after school started Judy got sick and had to stay home. She complained of her leg hurting. Then she began to look drawn and seemed too tired by bedtime. I took her to the doctor, but he said there wasn't anything wrong and suggested maybe it was her way of getting attention. But I watched Judy when she didn't know I was watching. She would run after Vicki and her friends, trying to keep up, and would drag her left leg. I knew something was wrong.

Through prayer and dreams that sometimes turned into nightmares, my anxiety continued until I took her back to the doctor and insisted that he X-ray that leg. That was when he found Perthes' disease. I had never heard of it until then. The only treatment then known was to take the weight off her leg. To do that, she would have to wear a harness and walk on crutches until the hip healed. The doctor had no idea how long it would take.

Even more baffling, she suddenly developed a high temperature that the doctor could not explain. It was not a symptom of Perthes' disease. She'd had only a very slight temperature before, along with cold sweats at night. Fear struck at my heart as I stood beside her bed and watched her little body getting increasingly weaker. She was so thin that her ribs and hip bones were almost coming through the skin. And she was so hot that it was as if she were burning up from the inside.

Nothing we did seemed to help. She became delirious and began talking about Heavenly Father, and she seemed to have lost the will to fight. It was then, as I knelt beside her bed, that I remembered that she really belonged to Heavenly

Father and that he had only lent her to us. I prayed and told him that I would give her back to him if he needed her, if I had to. All I asked was that if she had to go, he would somehow find a way to help me bear her loss.

We were blessed. The next morning Judy's temperature was down and she was covered with red spots. Now the doctor knew what was wrong: she'd had measles with her Perthes'. Never had I been so grateful for red spots. I knew Heavenly Father had let her stay with us, and the pain of almost losing her eased the fear of the problems associated with Perthes' disease.

When Judy was well enough to be out of bed, we took her to be fitted for the harness and crutches she would have to wear. That day was burned into my memory forever. The harness, made of heavy cloth straps, was put on like a jacket, under her clothes. Then her left leg, with the knee bent, was pulled up and attached to the harness with buckles at her back.

She stood silently, on one foot, while she was measured and her crutches were fit to her hands and under her arms. Then, when the harness and crutches were finished, she looked down at herself. I wanted to cry, but I made myself smile brightly. "Judy, aren't they the cutest little crutches you've ever seen in your life?"

She just kept looking down at herself. Finally she looked up at me, and said, "Will you carry me to the car, Mom?"

I lifted her into my arms and carried her, crutches and all, to the car. When we got home, she sat on the couch where she had been sitting so long, and I put her crutches beside her in case she wanted to try to use them. Then I went into the kitchen.

She was tired of sitting, but even though she hadn't cried or said anything about them, I knew she had decided she wouldn't use those crutches. However, before long I heard her get up and try them. She walked carefully around the front room on the carpet at first. Then I heard her peg down the hall, and finally she appeared in the kitchen. I was delighted and hugged her.

Judy walked around the house—too much for the first time, but when she started something, there wasn't any quitting. At last she stood by the outside door and asked me to open it.

"Don't you think you'd better wait until tomorrow to try the steps and going outside?" I asked.

She shook her head and waited. Judy didn't like having to stay in; that had been one of the hardest things of her illness. I opened the door and held it for her, and she made her way down the two steps and started toward the backyard. Then I heard her crutches hit the cement.

I ran to pick her up. She wasn't crying as I'd expected—not until she looked down and saw a little blood on her knee. Then she burst into tears. I held her in my arms and let her sob. I knew it wasn't the knee that really hurt.

That was the only time Judy ever cried about her crutches or what had happened to her. She fell asleep after she cried, and when she woke up she was back on her crutches again.

"They're fun, aren't they? Now you don't have to sit all the time," I said.

"Yes, Mom," she said quietly, "but I don't have to go to school with them, do I?"

I didn't know what I would do if she didn't go back to school, but I answered, "No, you don't have to go to school with them if you don't want to."

But Judy loved school, and the next morning she was up early and ready to go, crutches, harness, and all. And that day her new popularity started. Her classmates made a huge fuss over her when she entered her schoolroom. Even the two girls who had given her such a bad time greeted her at the door. Judy couldn't believe it. Everyone clamored around and wanted a turn to try out her crutches. After that it wasn't uncommon to see Judy hopping around on one leg while the children took turns on her crutches. Not to be left out, the children who gathered in our neighborhood for the school bus came to our house every day to give her a ride to the bus stop in her wagon, just so they could use her crutches.

For eighteen months the Perthes' was active. During that time Judy became an inspiration to her classmates and other children. Often I'd get phone calls from parents I'd never met, telling me how much Judy had done for their children. One mother said her son had had his father whittle out some sticks to use as crutches so he could be like Judy.

When I went to school for a parents' program, I saw that Judy wasn't left out of anything. For the dances she had a partner, like everybody else. When she had to dance around her partner, she'd drop her crutches and hop around him, then pick them up and go on, never missing a beat.

One day in the park when Judy was staring at a woman who was grossly overweight, I told her that it wasn't nice to stare at people. "Why not?" Judy asked. "People stare at me."

With calluses worn on her hands and under her arms, Judy finally was healed enough to give up the crutches. And the very same day she cast them aside, she learned to roller skate and ride a bike. Yes, all in one day. The following Sunday, she stood up in sacrament meeting to thank Heavenly Father and everyone who had prayed for her to get well.

After the crutches, Judy took up modern dance rather than therapy. Her muscles had become strong enough to hold her hip bone so that she could walk without a limp, even though one leg was half an inch shorter than the other.

In junior high and high school, Judy was on the tumbling team. And in college, she majored in physical education and minored in dance so she could become a dance and school teacher. Her leg always hurt, and she could not do the splits or rotate her leg the way she wanted to as a dancer, but she seldom complained, and the pain never slowed her down.

When Judy got married, I worried that her hip would give her problems with childbirth, but it held through five births, all natural. The hip was, of course, wearing down, and she knew that someday she would have to have an operation. But she would not do it until the pain became unbearable, nor would she walk with a cane, as her doctor often suggested.

In the kitchen, as I prepared Derek's lunch, my mind returned to the present, and I wondered what was happening with this new pain of Judy's. Then Neal called and told me the doctor wanted her to go to the hospital. She would undergo an operation the next morning to have the kidney stone removed.

Neal finally got home after the children and I had had dinner and had set up the movie projector for home movies. It was Monday, family night, and their parents had promised them they could see the movies.

Though Neal was very tired and seemed to be coming down with a cold, he insisted on watching half of the movies with the children. Then he cut Tucker's hair. It was late when we all finally climbed into bed.

Neal left for the hospital early the next morning. Then Tucker, Maren, Lyndsy, and Spencer went to school. Only Derek was left, until a friend's mother came to pick him up for preschool.

While I waited to hear from Neal, the phone rang a lot. Judy and Neal had a lot of friends, and many had already heard that she was in the hospital.

The carpenter came and finished some details, and I kept busy by moving the children's things back into their rooms. I picked up a little stool and saw that it was decorated with tole painting. One year for Christmas Judy had given her sisters and me some tole painting. When she turned domestic, she went all the way.

One day she came to see me and asked me to teach her how to crochet.

"Judy, I don't know much about crocheting," I said. "I sew on the sewing machine."

"But Mom, you used to make little skating outfits and sweaters for our dolls at Christmas."

"Yes, with a few stitches my mother taught me. I don't even know what they're called. I just do them."

"Show me how to do them."

So I showed her what I knew, and she picked it up fast. Not long after that, Judy showed me two shawls she had made. The stitches were far beyond anything I could do.

"How did you learn to do that?" I asked.

"I took a class at the university, and I bought a magazine on crocheting. It's easy, if you follow the directions."

Every year she gave some homemade things to her sisters for Christmas. I thought back to our last party.

Judy had arrived at Vicki's house with her gifts and a cooked turkey. She had wanted to prepare the turkey even though she hadn't been feeling well. She wore a bright new red dress, which made her look vibrant despite the dark circles around her eyes. She hadn't said anything, but her sisters and I had worried when she agreed to lie down on the couch to rest. That wasn't our Judy. Maybe the kidney stone was the problem.

It was late afternoon when Neal called to tell me the operation was over and Judy was back in her room.

"They didn't operate as early as they wanted to," he said. "There were some complications with her blood, and they had to give her three pints before they could operate and one more afterwards." He had returned to the candy factory, where Tucker had stopped after school. They would go to the hospital and stay with Judy until she was out of the anesthetic.

As I fixed dinner, my worries about Judy increased. That was a lot of blood for just a kidney-stone operation. But, I reasoned, she had said she was anemic.

When Neal and Tucker arrived home late that evening, Neal's cold was worse. And—was there something else? Looking at him, I got a deep, sick feeling in my stomach again, an intuition of impending danger. I brushed it off.

"Is she all right?" I asked Neal.

"We left her sleeping," he said.

"I've saved dinner. Are you hungry?"

"Not very . . . but I haven't eaten." He coughed as he sat down at the table, but he didn't seem to be interested in food.

"Maybe you need rest more than food," I said.

A little later, while I was standing in Maren's room where I'd gone to hang up something, Neal came to the door. He seemed to hesitate; then finally he said, "After Judy's operation, they found something else." I looked at him quickly as he continued. "When she was in such pain and didn't respond the way they expected, they did a bone-marrow test. They found out she has . . . cancer."

My heart stopped as I stared at him. Cancer! Memories of past pain flooded my mind, mingled with the devastating implications of what the future might bring. I didn't cry—I just stood and stared at Neal.

At last I said, "Are they sure?" But even as I asked the question, I knew that Neal wouldn't have said such a thing if it weren't true.

"Does she know?" I finally said.

"No. I haven't told her yet. They have some more tests to take."

I'm not sure what happened during the next few hours. It was as if a black cloud had settled over me and I was only partly hearing, partly feeling. I wanted to say or do something to help Neal, to comfort him, but anything I thought of seemed totally inadequate.

Neal and the children finished looking at the home movies. One scene showed Judy on the way to the hospital to have Tucker. She was trying to get Neal to put away the camera and hurry to the hospital because her labor pains were becoming stronger. I wished she was only having labor pains now.

Later, when everyone was in bed, I called my husband, Milt. Neal had said he didn't want to tell anybody—not even the children—until the doctors were sure about the diagnosis, but I had to let Milt know why I wouldn't be coming home that night. When Milt asked about Judy, I mumbled something about complications and I think I mentioned the word *cancer*, but I told him not to call anyone, just pray.

After hanging up the receiver I went to bed, but I knew it would take more than going to bed to turn off the turmoil in my mind. As I tossed and turned, trying to warm up my cold feet, all I could think about was getting home to Milt and calling my daughters. I wanted to tell them the news before they called the hospital and found out.

CHAPTER 2

The phone rang early the next morning. I picked it up in the kitchen at the same time Neal picked up an extension downstairs. I heard Judy's voice ask, "Neal, am I going to die?"

Just those words, and I knew the doctor had broken the news to her. Mechanically I hung up the receiver and started to prepare breakfast and sack lunches for the children. They appeared one at a time to eat breakfast, pick up their lunches, have a quick prayer, and leave for school. Derek was in his room, playing with his toys.

Neal came into the kitchen after the children left, ready to return to the hospital. He sat down to the breakfast I had prepared and tried to eat but couldn't. Finally he said, "Judy called this morning. She asked me if she was going to die."

"What did you tell her, Neal?"

"I said I hoped not." He stared into space for a few moments, then said, "She's already had so much pain in her life. It doesn't seem fair."

"Do they want to give her chemotherapy?" I asked.

He nodded. "They want to start it right away."

"Oh, Neal, I don't want her to suffer! If she can live, then it would be worth the suffering, but if she can't, I don't want her to go through all that pain and hurt . . . "

He nodded again. "Whatever is best for Judy, that's what I want," he said.

I sensed the words he didn't say from the sag of his shoulders. I thought how much he and Judy depended on each other. They were a good team, each supplementing the other. My thoughts were racing.

"Neal, all my life I have prayed, studied, and searched for answers to help my children. I haven't done very well, have I."

"You've done the best you could."

"I know." I wanted to cry. I wanted Neal to cry, but neither of us could. I was so tight inside, so frightened, that my body wouldn't relax enough to cry.

"Do the doctors know any more this morning?"

"Judy has myeloblastic leukemia. The doctor says it is fast moving, but doctors have found help for treating leukemia in the past few years, and he is hopeful."

"What kind of help?"

"Chemotherapy first. Then, when she's in remission, she can have a bone-marrow transplant. They've had some success—more than with other kinds of cancer. We'll need a donor. It has to be a brother or sister."

His words threw another fear into me. Two children in the hospital? A quick vision passed in front of my eyes, a vision of me sitting in the hospital watching Judy go through . . . what would she have to go through? Would it be a repeat performance of the weeks my son, Devro, spent in the hospital with his wife and son, those difficult weeks when we had all watched them both die? Devro's eyes still showed the scars of that emotional crisis. Now he had Lori and their boys; his life had been put back together. But Neal . . . Judy and Neal had been together for seventeen and a half years.

Ever since I had almost died when Loni, our youngest, was born, I had prayed that I wouldn't linger and have to have my loved ones watch me die. I don't know why, but I had thought about that a lot. I had warned my husband and children that they were not to hold on to me because I didn't want them to go through that. I always hoped that if I did all I could in my life, I would be spared that. I wanted to go quickly when my time came. Perhaps everyone does, though we may deny ourselves blessings by feeling that way.

Yet, it had never occurred to me then that I might be the one to watch others suffer and die. If this had to happen to Judy . . . Why couldn't I take her place? I had lived my life, raised my children. But experience had taught me that bargaining didn't do any good. Everyone has a right to his or her own blessings, no matter how difficult they are to earn. This would be a blessing, I knew, even though I didn't like the odds of what I knew and didn't know about cancer.

Neal's cold was still bad when he left to go to the hospital, and my heart ached for him. I hurt for Judy, too, and dreaded telling her sisters and brother.

I hurried to straighten the house so I could drive home and back before the children got home from school. Judy called just before I was ready to leave. "Mom, I don't want this," she said. "I don't want the chemo or the cancer or any of this. It isn't fair. I've got too much to do to go through all this."

"I know, Judy. I wish I knew the answers. All I can think of to tell you is that when I went to the Holy Land and stood in the Garden of Gethsemane, I knew that it was just an ordinary garden, with olive trees that are old and not as pretty as most gardens I've seen. But there was a special feeling there, and I was moved because I remembered that an innocent brother of ours was there once too. He didn't want to go through what he had to do either, but he did." As I said the words to Judy, I realized I was listening to them myself, and they helped.

There was a silence on the phone a minute, and then Judy said, "I think Neal knows if I'm going to die or not and he won't tell me."

"I don't think so, Judy, not yet. He hasn't really had a chance to prepare himself or to pray in depth."

"He always gets answers. I know he knows and is afraid to tell me. Do you think I'm going to die, Mom?"

"Judy, I don't know. We have to do all we can to get you well."

"But what do you think?"

"I'm remembering that I gave you back to Heavenly Father once before, when you were little and so sick I thought you couldn't make it. He let you stay then; maybe he'll let you stay again."

"I've got to raise my family, Mom. I'm not ready to die. But if I'm going to go, I just want to get on with it." That was Judy—no fooling around, just get the job done.

"Judy, we're all praying for you. You have to have faith. I'm sure you'll be guided—"

"I've got to hang up, Mom," she interrupted. "The doctor's here."

"Judy, I'm going home to change and then I'm coming up to the hospital. And don't worry about the children, all right?"

"All right. Thanks, Mom."

I drove home, and all the way Judy's voice rang in my ears: "Neal knows and he's afraid to tell me."

Judy had always had a lot of faith in Neal's prayers. He had a gift of obedience and preparing himself, and he got the answers. More than that, when he got the answers he had the courage to follow them even if he didn't understand. I remembered when they were first married and Judy came to ask my advice about something. I said, "Why don't you pray about that, Judy; your knees bend as well as mine." And she just said happily, "Oh no, Neal's praying about it. He always gets answers and I don't. I'll just wait and see what he says."

Worried about how to tell Judy's sisters, I drove to Vicki's place first. I knew that her children had gone to school and she would be getting ready to go to work. I knocked and heard her call to me, and I made my way to the sound of her voice. She was just getting out of the shower.

"Mom, how's Judy?" she asked.

I shook my head a little, wondering how to tell her with the least pain.

"Mom?" She knew something was wrong, so I just said it.

"There are complications, Vicki. She has cancer."

"Oh, Mom!" Vicki broke down, with her tears flowing freely. "Mom, I'm not prepared to lose Judy. We can't!"

She put her arms around me and cried, and it was as if she were a little girl again, with each of us trying to comfort the other. I told her all I knew while she went on crying.

"Poor little Judy. I just can't stand this."

Cancer was new to us, and it was a word that had always meant no hope. And even though the doctor had told Neal this was the type that responded best to treatment, I didn't feel that he was telling us the whole story.

When I left Vicki's, I went to Linda's home. It was a repeat performance, except that after Linda had cried a little and asked a lot of questions, she began thinking of ways she might help Judy. As we talked, her doorbell rang. It was Vicki.

"I can't go to work," she explained. "I wouldn't be any good there. I want to go to the hospital with you, Mom."

She ran to keep an appointment while I showered and changed clothes. Then we drove to Judy's house to pick up Derek, who was out of school and staying with a friend. We picked him up and then drove to the hospital.

Milt met us at the hospital. Derek couldn't go in Judy's room, so Vicki and I took turns staying in the lobby with him. I went to see Judy first. She didn't look well. She was in a lot of pain but was doped up.

"Mom," she said, trying to smile. "Mom, I'm not ready to die."

"I don't suppose any of us are," I replied. "But you don't have to make that decision yet. Let's just think about letting Heavenly Father make those decisions—trust him."

I put my arms around her as best I could and tried to reassure her about the odds of getting well. Finally I said, "Vicki is downstairs with Milt and Derek. I'm going down so they can come up. Think positive, Judy."

"I'll try, Mom." She managed a half smile, and I kissed her and left.

Vicki had bought Derek a toy to play with, and I sat with him while Vicki went up to see Judy. She had brought Judy a Madame Alexander doll, "Pinkie." Judy was a doll collector and knew the value of Pinkie.

"Now I know I'm going to die," she told Vicki, "or you wouldn't have brought me the doll."

That night I called Loni, our youngest daughter, in Washington. I hated to tell her about Judy because she was alone, but she knew something was wrong by the sound of my voice.

"I want to be there with you," she said after I explained what had happened. She was already planning to come in the summer for a dance class at Brigham Young University, so I said, "It won't be long now. Isn't it a blessing you had already decided to come?"

"But it's so long! If she isn't better soon, I'll change my reservation and come immediately."

"I'll let you know," I told her.

"Do, Mom, please do." Then her voice changed. "Mom, she isn't going to die. We aren't going to let her die."

"Pray for her, Loni. We need your prayers."

"I will, Mom."

When I called Devro to tell him, there was a silence and then he asked, "What's the treatment?" I told him about the possibility of a bone-marrow transplant.

"I'll be the donor," he said.

"But all four of you will have to be tested. The donor will be the one whose marrow matches."

"I'll match. I know I'll be the donor."

"We don't have to decide that yet. The first thing is to get her into remission."

"I'll be ready, Mother. I want to do it for her."

As I hung up the phone, I realized how hard this was on Devro. A few years ago, in the same hospital, he had spent several weeks in the intensive-care room while he watched his wife and son die. How could he handle another episode in that hospital?

I stayed with Judy's children that night so Neal could go to the hospital. The next morning she called again.

"Mom, they've moved me into the cancer section. Everybody here looks at me and shakes their head like they know I'm going to die."

"That won't be their decision, Judy," I said firmly.

"Mom, I've got to have somebody in the hospital with me all the time, either you or Neal. It's so frightening."

"I'll come, Judy, anytime you want me. I just thought you wanted me with the children."

"We've got to make other arrangements for the children. I can't face these things alone."

Silently I said a prayer of gratitude that Judy would ask for help, that she knew her strength and her limitations, and that I didn't have to guess where she wanted me or how I could help.

Neal talked to the children, and they took it very well. They spoke to their mother on the phone every day, and to them she didn't sound any different. I knew they didn't realize the seriousness of what she was going through, and I decided that was another blessing.

I also spent a lot of time on the phone. The news had gotten around, and many people called. Neal was bishop of his ward and part-owner of a candy company. He and Judy were two people who always stayed busy, and each of their five children had a schedule to match. Judy had made temporary arrangements for the children to find rides to their many activities for the few days she had expected to be in the hospital. Now she had to make more permanent ones. She handled those arrangements from the hospital.

I felt better when I was in the hospital with Judy. Watching her was difficult, but worrying about her when I was away was much more wearing. She was very sick. She had to have help to get out of bed and to walk across the room to the bathroom. She was still hurting from the kidney operation. She slept on and off, and once as she reached for my hands she clung to me and, with a frightened look in her eyes, said, "You'll get me well, won't you, Mom? You always get me well."

Her words stayed with me. As I watched her, I thought again of those eighteen long months of Perthes' disease, how we'd searched for answers when the doctors didn't have any, how we'd learned to trust each other and to pray together. Here we were again, and once again I didn't have any answers.

Patience isn't one of my best qualities. I've learned to make friends with patience a few times, such as when I lost my mother in a train accident a week before Judy was born. But waiting with no action is difficult for me. And Judy? Judy didn't even know the meaning of the word. To Judy, patience was something she was going to have when she got older. Ever since she was little, she had been our goer, energetic and athletic. She grew up but had never grown taller than four feet ten and a half inches. I remembered that all she wanted for Christmas as a teenager was to be five feet tall. That was the only goal she had never reached.

Now, as Judy began to feel a little better, she filled me in on some details of what had been happening to her while I was with her children.

"When I left you that morning, Mom, and I was in so much pain, Neal took me to the doctor's office first. But the pain didn't stop, so the doctor gave me a shot. You know what drugs do to me. I started vomiting, and that made me very weak, so we decided to have the operation and do any further tests at the hospital."

The kidney-stone operation had three parts to it, she explained. First the doctor inserted a catheter. Then he inserted a tube in her back through which he would do the surgery. He also told Judy that even if an ultrasound instrument were available in Salt Lake City, her kidney stone was so large that it was probably better to remove it surgically.

"They inserted the tube into my back and pushed it on into the kidney and explained that it had to be lined up perfectly with the kidney stone," she continued. "My kidney was so swollen and the kidney stone so large that they had a difficult time lining it up. What should have been a twenty-minute procedure took over an hour. They gave me only a local anesthetic, and it was very painful. The doctor sat by me and held my hand through the whole thing and kept telling me to squeeze his hand. That really helped."

The third part of the operation, Judy told me, came when she was wheeled into the operating room to have the kidney stone removed. The anesthesiologist told her that because she had a cold, she ran a risk of getting pneumonia. But because it was an emergency, they would have to take that risk.

"Then they took the blood test you were too sick to have the day before?" I asked.

"Yes, and my blood count was low. The operation was scheduled for early morning, but I wasn't rolled into the operating room until about two thirty, because my blood was so low that I had to take three pints of blood before they could operate. After the operation they gave me one more pint of blood."

"Judy, that was what worried me. I knew you were supposed to go in early, and when Neal didn't call—"

"Oh, Mom, I've never had an operation before, and I woke up in so much pain. It frightened me. I didn't know there could be so much pain! The pain in my back was intense and my stomach was bloated. I was awfully thirsty and they wouldn't give me any water, just sponges dipped in ice water, to wash my mouth."

"Oh, Judy, I know about operations. There's no way to explain the pain, but once you've had one you never forget. They gave you something for the pain, didn't they?"

"Yes, and it spaced me out. They took me to my room and Tucker and Neal were there, but I can't remember very much except how much I hurt. Neal said he asked me if I recognized them and I told him, 'Oh, shut up!' Then I heard Tucker say, 'It's Mom, Dad. She's got her old fight back.' I guess Tucker realized how sick I'd been before I went to the hospital. After that the painkillers took over and I slept through the night."

"You needed the sleep," I assured her.

"But I woke up with pneumonia."

"And Neal has it too. He had a shot today, so maybe he can throw it off."

"He's got to get better because I need him. He has to be here to help make decisions. I don't want to be hurt without you or Neal here with me." Her words tore at my heart.

"Neal is half sick and yet he's trying to be a good bishop, an excellent father, a perfect executive, and a husband," I said. "He can't keep that up. He's ill himself."

"He's got to get some sleep, Mom."

"Yes, Judy, I know . . . " *But Neal is his own person,* I said to myself. *He does what he has to do no matter what anyone says.*

CHAPTER 3

When the chemotherapy treatments were started, Neal and I were with Judy. That was the night her cousin Jeddy came to see her. Jeddy was leaving town on an important business trip, but he felt that he had to come to the hospital first. He had lost his twelve-year-old son the preceding November, and he knew how important it was to show his personal concern.

When Jeddy arrived, Judy's room was already full, so he waited. I stood there and thought about Judy and Jed. They had been in and out of each other's lives from the time they were little. During their dating years, they had sometimes called on each other when they needed a partner for a special event and didn't want to date one of their own crowd.

On one of those dates he had taken her to a ward dance. She was so short, and he so tall, that he had put her up on a step of the stage in the cultural hall while he stood on the floor below to dance with her. They had attracted a lot of attention, and it was a night of fun and laughs. Jeddy was also Neal's friend. They had grown up in the same ward and gone to the same schools.

When the others left, Jeddy came closer and sat beside Judy's bed. But just as they started to talk, the nurse came in to give her some medication.

"This is going to make me sleepy and I'm not ready to be sleepy," she told him. "Will you wait and help Neal give me a blessing? And Mom," she said, still very much in charge, "if I get sleepy, I want you to listen to every word and tell me in the morning what they said." She reached up and took Neal's hand. "Neal," she said, her eyes shining and pleading at the same time, "a little miracle, please, a little miracle. Get me well."

It was a beautiful blessing. Neal prayed for the doctors who attended her and the nurses who would be with her, and that the decisions they made would be in her best interests. He prayed for the children, and that Judy would be comforted and know they were all right. He said many more things, but not that she would be immediately healed. Judy heard it all and was satisfied. She smiled, and with tears in her eyes she thanked Neal and Jeddy and talked a little while before she fell asleep.

Over the next few days the phone calls continued, flowers started arriving, and members of the Relief Society brought food to Judy's house. I stayed with the children when Neal was at the hospital. And I went to see Judy as often as I could, but there wasn't a lot I could do for her. I could rub her feet, talk to her visitors when she was asleep, answer the phone, and try to keep her mind off what she was going through. I could help her walk down the hall with her tubes attached to a hanger, and several times throughout the day and night, I would wake her to use her breather exerciser, which the doctor said was necessary to keep her lungs open.

"Mom," she said one evening as we tried to arrange the pillows so she would be more comfortable, "I've got pneumonia, I've just had a kidney-stone operation, and I've got cancer. I wonder what else I can get?"

"Just put yourself in Heavenly Father's hands," I said.

"I know I can get well, Mom," she responded, "but it's just . . . what do I have to do to make it?"

Friends, friends, and more friends. Judy was showered with presents. Her room looked like a florist's shop, and she had more phone calls than she could answer. One friend who visited said he knew Judy was going to get well because she had her makeup on.

That was Judy. She always tried to look good. She wore her rings and earrings, dressed in colorful nightgowns, robes, and slippers, and had a good attitude. But one thing worried her: Would she lose her hair? at least, that worried her until she found other worries more important.

"The first part of the chemo," she told me, "is the part that takes a person's hair out. It doesn't take it right away, but it's the chemical that affects the hair. I might be blessed not to lose it, Mom—but I'm not planning on it."

Judy had such beautiful red hair. I remembered when I was pregnant with her, and Milt and I had wondered what she would look like. Vicki, our firstborn, had dark hair and eyes. "What do you want this time?" I had asked Milt.

"Girl or boy, I don't care which, or if she has red hair, a freckled face, and buck teeth—just as long as she's healthy and gets here."

He had said "she" as if he knew we were going to have another girl, or maybe because he had enjoyed Vicki so much that he really wanted another girl.

And Judy was born with red hair—no freckles or buck teeth, but lots of red hair. She was very tiny, just a little over five pounds, and her skin was like velvet. She was a favorite of the nurses on the hospital obstetric floor, and they showed her off to everyone.

Judy was vain, in her own way, always wanting to look just right. She had learned to style her own hair and did it most of the time. I wondered how she would respond to not having hair. How would her husband and children respond?

"Mom?"

"Yes, Judy."

"I told Vicki that I thought losing my hair would be worse than dying. But Mom, it won't really be that bad. I want to live so badly, it just doesn't matter about my hair."

"Of course not."

"And Sandy said (Sandy was Judy's cousin and her hair stylist) it's no big thing nowadays. She said there are such pretty wigs, no one will even know. 'Only your hairdresser will know for sure,' she told me."

Fighting for her life had changed a lot of Judy's priorities.

There were many difficult things to endure in addition to the recovery from an operation and cancer complications. The morning she was scheduled for a Hickman line insertion (a permanent line into her chest so the nurses wouldn't have to keep inserting needles), the intern came in early. Neither Neal nor I had arrived yet. He told her that the procedure was fairly simple and wouldn't hurt. So Judy let him go ahead. By the time I got to the hospital she was shaking and still crying.

"It hurt so much, Mom. They didn't give me anything for pain—and it hurt!" I held her hand tightly as she explained the details. "The intern couldn't get it in right, he just kept probing. I cried and cried. I was a basket case."

"I'm so sorry I wasn't here. I should have come early."

"I'd have called, Mom, but he said it wouldn't hurt. I'm not going to let anyone do anything to me anymore unless you or Neal can be here."

Judy's intolerance for drugs and medications made her wary, and she checked out each one before she took any. "Drugs make me vomit. I'm not used to them," she told the nurses and interns. "Don't give me any that I don't absolutely have to have."

Her stand was pretty clearly understood by the nurses after the first few days, but she and I laughed about an intern who came in every night to see if she needed any drugs or soft drinks. She always said no, and the intern always seemed surprised, maybe even a little distressed, that she didn't order anything. Judy was aware of good nutrition; she thought a lot about her body and what went into it.

Neal and I were both with her when the kidney-stone tube was taken out. The doctor let Neal stand beside her and hold her hand while a nurse gave her a shot of morphine in her back to deaden the pain. The moment the drug hit her, she started to vomit. Finally, as the numbness took effect, the doctor asked us both to step outside while he took the tube out. This time the nurse held her hand. Judy had always insisted on holding hands for comfort.

While we waited outside her room, I remembered a time in Yellowstone Park, when we were camping out and the weather suddenly turned cold. Everyone was clamoring for my attention—all but Judy. When I finally got everyone bedded down in sleeping bags and extra blankets and sweaters, I made one last check. There was little Judy shivering in her sleeping bag, wearing only a cotton summer nightshirt. I pulled her close to me and cuddled her cold little body in my arms. She reached for my hand, held it tight, and went back to sleep.

Now, outside Judy's hospital room, Neal and I sat together and waited. His head was bowed, and I supposed he was praying, as I was. It seemed as if all I did was pray. Father in heaven was the only one who I felt knew what was really going on, and I desperately needed his help and the comfort of the Holy Ghost.

Finally we were allowed to go back into Judy's room. "It hurt only a little," she told us. "It helped to have my nurse's hand to squeeze. But now I'm spaced out with morphine. I guess I'll have to sleep. It's nice to have the tube out. Maybe I can sleep on my back without it hurting now."

One morning I arrived at the hospital to find Judy sitting in a chair beside her bed, reading a letter. She was crying.

"What is it, Judy?" I asked anxiously.

"Mom, everyone says I'm so strong," she said. "But I'm not. I don't want to be."

"I know, Judy, but you are."

"Am I, Mother?"

"Of course you are. You've been making wise decisions all your life. I've watched you become strong because of the choices you've made."

"I don't feel strong," she said. "I feel like I'm being punished."

"What for?"

"I don't know. And why me?" She looked at the letter in her hands. As she folded and replaced it in the envelope, she said, "This says I'm such an example . . . I don't want to be an example."

"I know, Judy. You said that once before, when you were in junior high. Don't you remember?" She shook her head. "It was when you were elected vice-president of the student body in the eighth grade. You came home feeling so unhappy. You were glad to be elected, but a girl you didn't know had accused you of thinking you were too good because you hadn't said hello to her in the hall."

"I didn't know all those kids, Mom."

"Of course you didn't. But they knew you. And then I tried to explain that they expected you to be the example. Do you remember what you said?"

"That I didn't want to be an example. I just wanted to be me."

"Right. And you cried. And then—"

"And then, Mom, you said, 'Judy, we're all examples even if we don't want to be, either for good or bad.' I remember, but I still don't like it. And now this," she said, referring to the letter she had just read. "Mom, so many people are so good to me."

I looked at her and smiled. "That's because you've been good to them. And you are strong, Judy. It might be easier to be weak, but you aren't."

Judy didn't spend a lot of time talking or philosophizing. She just acted on her feelings. She was always doing, not talking. I remembered writing to her when she went to BYU. I always tried to say something wise, as a mother should. If it was something Judy could use, she understood on the first telling. If she couldn't use it, there was no use trying to say the same thing in a few more ways.

Judy handled her hospital days as she handled her life, doing what she had to do, accepting even what she couldn't understand, but asking questions. She had to know everything the medical personnel were doing or going to do, all the time. And she prayed about everything. If there was a big decision to make, she would call Neal at the candy factory and say, "Come over here, Neal, we've got to make some more decisions. I need your help and a blessing."

Judy's immediate goal was remission. Her long-range goal was to get well and return to what she had been doing. One big battle she fought constantly was her begrudging the time she had to spend in the hospital when she wanted to be doing so much elsewhere.

Neal and Judy lived only a few miles from the hospital, so she was able to talk often with the children. They could call whenever they needed her. When I was with her, I answered the phone, visited with her friends when too many had come or she was too tired to visit, sat in the chair beside her bed, made her warm herb drinks that helped settle her stomach, and prayed.

At first I thought Judy's hair wasn't going to come out at all. Every day she showered and washed it. Every day she put on her makeup and we walked in the halls. Every day she answered letters, wrote thank-you notes, watched videos, tried to sleep, and learned how to tolerate illness. But when her hair did come out, it came in handfuls. Then she put on a little scarf at night, wore wigs in the daytime, and went on as before.

Neal's work as bishop of the ward had kept him busy day and night for almost five years. But when Judy got sick, his counselors took over for him so he could be with her and with the children as much as possible. They pulled the ward together, and they all fasted and prayed for Judy.

One letter from her daughter's schoolteacher related an incident that brought tears to our eyes as Judy read it: "The children knew today was a fast for you, Judy. But of course no one expected children to fast. But at noon, two little girls, friends of Lyndsy, stayed in at noon and didn't eat their lunch because they were fasting for Lyndsy's mother."

Many people fasted that day and gathered at the ward when the fast was over. Many came to talk about the bishop and his wife and the inspiration they had been to others. The meeting was taped so Judy could listen to it later.

One little girl had said that Judy was going to be at the meeting. "Oh, I don't think so," said her mother, who had just visited Judy. "She's too sick to get out of the hospital."

"Then they'll bring her in an ambulance. I know she's going to be there, and I want to see her."

Judy listened to that report on the phone. "My big dramatic moment," she said, laughing. "I'll come in an ambulance and make an entrance. Can't you just see it?"

Visualizing wasn't difficult for Judy, who was an actress, dancer, and showman with lots of fans. She had always responded to applause and an audience. Her first performance as a tap dancer, I remembered, was when she and Vicki were on stage at Liberty Park before she started school. Judy was really just an ordinary dancer, but when the spotlight hit her—well, she was a showman. "She's a real ham," her aunt remarked as we watched her dance in time to the music.

And so she was. I remembered another time when she had tried out for a roadshow in our ward. I'd helped to write the show and told her there was a part that perfectly suited her talents. I had watched her perform around the house and knew what she could do.

"Just get up there and show them what you can do, loud and clear," I said.

"I'm not going to get up there and make a fool of myself," she replied.

When the tryouts were over, I told her, "You know, you could have had the part your friend got."

"I know," she said, the tears close to the surface, "and I could have done it better than she did if I'd tried."

"You know you could have done it better, and I know it, but the director didn't know it because you didn't show her."

Judy learned from that. The next year tryouts were held for the stake production of *Peter Pan*. Judy auditioned, and this time she really made a big fool of herself. She came home with the part of Peter Pan.

What a thrill that was! Judy, without any previous singing experience, sang eight solos in that show. After the curtain came down, someone said, "Judy, I didn't know you could sing." Her father, with his arm around her, couldn't resist saying, "Well, we're not kidding ourselves that you can sing, but you sure did shout cute."

We had another memorable experience with that play. As Peter Pan, Judy flew in through the center window, upstage, with a wire attached to her back and her foot held out like a dancer. As she swung out over the orchestra pit, up high on the side, and was on her way down to center stage to stand beside Wendy, the wire broke and let her down hard.

The audience gasped and stood up. Judy stood up too. She walked to the front of the stage and said, "I'm sorry I fell. If you'll just keep your seats, I'll do it again."

The curtains were drawn while the nylon rope holding the piano wire was fixed. As Judy waited, she realized the danger and cried a little, but when the pulley was ready, she said, "Now get me up again . . . higher this time."

She set the mood for the whole show. The rest of the cast rallied around her and were determined to be as good as she was. She inspired that kind of confidence in others.

Judy had a tenderness, too, that came out in all she did. Once, as the stepmother in *Cinderella* and playing the part with a vengeance, she pushed poor Cinderella and gave her a quick little kick of emphasis, just as she was supposed to do. But afterward she worried about that part. She didn't like to be mean to anyone.

Judy loved pets—dogs, cats, turtles, rabbits—anything but snakes. She brought home strays, sneaked them into the house when I wasn't looking, and always asked for more variety. She wanted a Saint Bernard dog because she had seen one and put her arms around it. And, of course, she wanted a chimpanzee. If Judy had been given free range, our house would have been turned into a zoo.

And Judy had a way of getting her father to do what she wanted him to do, often by mimicking his words. One night when she was only about two years old, Milt sat at the dinner table and made a list of items he needed to landscape the backyard.

"I need this" and "I need that," he was saying.

"I need a slickery slide," Judy said. We all laughed. But Judy got her slickery slide: the biggest in the neighborhood. And she used it. Little as she was, she climbed to the top of that big slide and slid to the bottom, all alone.

At last, after the chemo treatment ended and the nausea subsided, Judy's doctor came to take another bone-marrow test. This was the big moment. Neal and I were both there. We took hold of our faith and Judy's hands as the marrow sample was taken. Then we waited for the result.

When I arrived at the hospital the next day, Judy had already had her bath and was dressed in a pretty nightgown and robe. We talked a little, and I reported on the activities of her children and other family members. Then the phone rang. Judy answered, and when she hung up she burst into tears.

"That was the doctor, Mom," she said between sobs. "I'm in remission!"

We both cried, and then she called Neal at the candy company. But she was crying so hard she couldn't talk. I took the phone and said, "Hang on, Neal. These are happy tears."

"Neal! Neal!" she gasped. "I'm in remission!"

Later, when the tears subsided, she looked up at me from where she sat on the edge of her bed.

"I'm so grateful, Mom," she said, "so grateful to Heavenly Father. Let's have a prayer to thank him."

Together we knelt beside her bed, and she offered a sweet, humble prayer. In my heart I responded. The first part of her trip back to life was over. We had all been blessed.

CHAPTER 4

Remission! Judy couldn't wait to spread the news. The second person she called was her sister Linda. Again the tears came after the hello, and all Linda heard were the sobs. When Judy finally relayed the news, Linda said, "Judy, next time would you mind telling me if it's good news or bad first and then cry. I almost had a heart attack."

Happy news! Remission had been the only thing in our minds for so long that we thought the victory was won. What we didn't realize until later was that the hard part was just beginning. Now Judy had to rebuild her immune system. A sterile sign was put on the door to her hospital room, and we sprayed our hands before entering.

We all went through the experience with her—both of Judy's families, because Neal's family was just like her own. They were there, supporting her, bringing her gifts, calling her on the phone, and laughing and crying with her. All of us suffered and all of our lives were affected daily. We all wanted to be in on the healing.

Linda tended Judy's children whenever she could, and Vicki had practically adopted Derek. He had visited her and her husband, Richard, often and felt very comfortable with them.

It was difficult for those who lived out of state and couldn't have daily updates or contact with Judy, as the rest of us did. I called family members when there was anything significant to report, but it wasn't like the hour-by-hour calls I made to Vicki and Linda, who lived close by.

I knew that Loni especially was suffering with Judy. A dancer like Judy, she identified with Judy and looked up to her. I remembered the time Judy took part in a melodrama in Park City, when Loni was a little girl. Loni was so proud to see Judy on the stage that she insisted on sitting beside her all the way home.

Devro was the one I worried about most. Judy's illness and hospitalization had reopened healing wounds for him, and I felt his suffering.

And me? I walked with Vicki whenever I wasn't in the hospital with Judy. Vicki and I walked and talked, and she cried. Vicki and Judy were closer together in age than any of our other children. As children they had even dressed alike. For a long time there had been only the four of us—Milt, me, Vicki, and Judy. The other three children came later and were well spaced, resulting in a twenty-year span between Vicki, number one, and Loni, number five.

Our talk while walking consisted mostly of Judy. We knew the odds of her surviving this kind of cancer, and even though she was in remission, we were a long way from knowing that the disease was gone.

"I'm not prepared to give Judy up, Mother," Vicki told me.

"That won't be our choice. We need to pray for what is best for Judy," I responded. "Being positive does not mean hanging onto her at all costs."

"What could be more important and better for her than raising her children and being with her husband?"

"Nothing, unless she could do all that from the other side more effectively than she can here. A greater calling is not always understandable."

"I don't want to believe that."

"Neither do I, but I still want what is best for Judy and that means leaving her in Heavenly Father's hands, according to the choices she made before she came here."

We had thought remission was not merely our goal, but the end of the fears and the worst of the illness past. But remission, we began to learn, was only the beginning of more difficult times.

Since the chemotherapy had killed all Judy's immunities, the big danger now was that she might get a germ or start bleeding before her body made its own blood and white platelets. Waiting for that process was even more difficult than the treatments with chemicals that killed everything.

Judy received blood transfusions and red platelets. Whenever she needed either, she would go through periods of depression and feel like crying a lot.

"Remember, your blood is low right now," Neal would remind her. "Don't try to make any decisions or expect to have a lot of energy. Just sleep and wait."

Then she'd receive some blood or platelets and she'd bounce back smiling and energetic again. She looked good. Her color was good. But it was difficult waiting for her body to build her blood so she could go home. Another concern was that she constantly had a little temperature. It wouldn't take much of an infection for us to lose her. The doctor thought she might be getting a little infection from her Hickman line, so he had it removed and needles were put back in her arms. The needles frightened her, and she called Neal.

"Neal, come . . . I need another blessing today, please."

Neal came, they talked, and then he gave her a blessing. He said a lot of things, and she was afraid he might forget the needles, so she interrupted him to remind him: "Needles, Neal, needles."

"And bless Judy," he prayed with his hands on her head and with full priesthood authority, "that she will think of the needles as her friends."

She did think of them as her friends from that moment on. After Neal said those words, the fear and the pain of those needles in her arms disappeared, and she slept.

It was difficult to carry on a normal home life. Every morning when I awakened it took me a few minutes to orient myself and decide where I was. Worse than that was the daily, terrible realization that it wasn't all a bad dream. Judy was still in the hospital, suffering and frightened, and her little family was still waiting for her to come home.

Sometimes I lay awake in bed and thought about Judy and Neal: Neal so positive, Judy so courageous, and the love they shared so intense. Theirs had been a storybook romance.

Being a dramatist, and coming from a home where gospel standards were taught and lived, I had seen and been part of blessings I believed had to be earned. I had raised the girls on tales of Cinderella and Beauty and the Beast, and had taught each that if she was to have a prince, she must make herself worthy and be a princess. Judy's friends often teased her about living for her prince to come along, but live that way she did, without compromise, fighting each battle as it came along. And Neal had been her prince.

Of course, she didn't recognize him right at first, going to college in his two-year-old missionary suits, driving an old beat-up car, being somewhat bashful and reserved. He was the typical person the old cliché described: truly a diamond in the rough. Judy was a member of a smart crowd, going with young men who knew how to dress well, who were outgoing, and who were considered outstanding men on campus. If she had been less of a princess, Neal might have been dethroned before she ever noticed his armor.

Removing the Hickman line did not take away the temperature; the doctors found no infection there. It had to be something else. Judy's doctor called in a specialist, and they decided she might need to take a new chemical antibiotic, one that was still in the experimental stage. It was frightening. They weren't sure of the side effects or if it could cause more problems than it helped. And they weren't sure it would solve the problem. There were no guarantees. The doctors were just doing what they felt best. It would be a drain on Judy's body, yet they were afraid not to give it to her.

"Come, Neal," Judy said on the phone. "We've got some more decisions to make."

Neal came, and by the time I got to the hospital, he and Judy had already had their prayers for guidance to make the decision. Neal had prepared himself, had become as knowledgeable about the situation as possible, and had gotten his answer.

"We'll wait on this one, Judy," he said.

"But Neal, are you sure? It could mean my life. The doctor said it was dangerous to wait."

"Judy, we prayed and got the answer. What good does it do to ask if we don't have the faith to follow the answer we receive?"

"But are you sure, Neal? You have to be sure. And what will my doctor say? He'll think I've lost faith in him. He won't be my doctor anymore, and I can't be without him. Neal, you have to be sure."

I couldn't tell just what Neal was thinking. He stood calm and firm. Judy was visibly shaken. But when I heard what the doctors wanted her to do, I was just plain panicked. A pain hit the pit of my stomach and wouldn't leave. All the old fears and visions surrounding the death of Devro's first wife came back. Was I to have to go through the same thing with Judy? Not again, oh, not again. Try this, try that—was this another experiment, and would it end the same way?

"But sometimes a fever means the body is fighting the infection," I said. "When you children were sick, a fever was usually a good sign that your bodies were fighting back."

"But not for me, Mom," Judy replied. "I haven't anything to fight with."

"How do you know that?"

"Because my immune system is gone. It hasn't come back
yet."

"How do the doctors know?"

"Mom . . . " I was upsetting Judy. I couldn't do that.
She knew what I was feeling. I had kicked off my shoes
when I sat down, and now I reached down to put them back
on.

"Mom, don't go. I'm sorry if I've hurt your feelings. Don't
go yet."

"Oh, no, Judy. It isn't my feelings. You couldn't possibly
hurt my feelings." She was sitting on the bed, and I went
over behind her and rubbed her shoulders. I couldn't let her
be concerned about me too, with all she was facing. But I
knew I had to get out of there—and do it without her thinking I was angry at her. Angry? How could I ever be angry at
Judy?

"Judy," I said, with my hand on her back transmitting
my love and concern, "I'm not good for you right now. This
decision is not mine, and I'm not rational on the subject of
experimental drugs. This will be a hard choice for you and
Neal, and you don't need any outside influence. I'll come
back later."

I walked from the room shakily, thinking that something
had happened to my equilibrium and wondering if I was
going to fall completely apart. Those other long weeks with
Dev's wife in the hospital . . . "Oh, Father in heaven," I
pleaded, "don't let this be a repeat. Don't let Judy go through
all that. Don't let us watch it happen again. There has to be
another way, a way without using experimental drugs."

I got in my car and backed it out of the parking lot. It
was raining. As I turned onto the freeway, just a few blocks
away, my mind was filled with Judy. Though she didn't always
understand Neal's gift of prayer and his answers, she trusted
him. Like Cinderella, who deserved her prince because she

had loved and served those who hated her, Judy had earned her prince through the decisions of her life and her hours of diligent work and service.

All around me the rain splashed, and the sound of it shut out the noise of oncoming cars. I felt as if I were all alone, free of the hurts beyond the doors of my car, out of the rain. I thought back to Judy's life and the events that had brought Neal into her life and made him her husband.

One scene that flashed into my mind was a high school dance that had been a trial to Judy. Her date was a boy who wasn't particularly her favorite, but he was nice—and he *had* asked her early.

The dance was formal, and for Judy, that meant sewing. We could never find a formal dress to fit her small, shapely body. She also had a problem with shoes. Her size, four and a half narrow, was usually the size of sample shoes. Sometimes we could get a pair on sale, but usually we paid full price—and such shoes were not inexpensive. So whenever Judy had to have a new dress and shoes, we established the budget and bought the shoes, and then with whatever was left, we would design a dress and I would sew.

This time, because the right boy had been too slow in asking, Judy wasn't excited about the dance. She still wanted to go, but every day she complained—complained that she'd been asked early and that she hadn't had a good excuse or a graceful or kind way to refuse. I started the dress late, and that didn't add to her good humor.

Just a few days before the dance, she came to me, asking, "Aren't you going to get my dress made, Mother?"

"That was the general idea when we spent money for the material."

"Well, you'd better get started." Her voice had just a tinge of bossiness, and I immediately became irritated. I was feeling guilty, too, that I had not been able to make the dress.

"Oh, I don't think there's a problem," I said evenly. "With the attitude you have about this dance and your date, you'll never have a good time anyway. Why don't you just wear one of your old ones and we'll make your new one for another time when your attitude will complement the dress?"

"I can't go to the dance without that dress," she insisted.

"Then maybe you shouldn't go," I countered. "You'll probably be doing the boy a favor if you tell him you're sick."

"You want me to lie to him?"

"No. Your personality is sick. You are not my happy Judy."

"I'm going to that dance. I'm in charge. So I've got to have the dress."

"You know how to sew—you make the dress." The mother in me was coming out, as always when I was pushed too far. "As of now, until you change your attitude, I am not touching that dress."

She didn't say much, and I knew she was depending on me to come through no matter what I said. But I held out. Two days before the dance, Judy went to school and I noticed she didn't talk very much that morning, but when she came home she was smiling.

"Mom, I'm going to that dance and I'm going to have a good time. It's my own fault I didn't have the right answers, so now I'm going, and I'll make sure he has a good time. You don't have to make the dress, Mom. I can wear one of my old ones. I'll be all right."

That was it. Judy did what she had to do—she changed her attitude—and so I did what I had to do. I made her dress and had it ready when she came home the next day. It was fun to do things for Judy when she was happy, and she was usually happy.

Often Judy drew pictures of styles of outfits she wanted and she expected me to make them, a task I was never sure I could accomplish. But she had a way of insisting, giving me confidence, and being excited and grateful when I came through, making me feel wonderful when I pleased her.

Judy had a lot of friends. Friends were always important to her, and in high school she was part of a group of young people who went everywhere together. The girls had grown up together and stuck together because they had the same interests, enjoyed the same activities, loved romance, studied hard, and weren't especially interested in getting serious with anyone.

Eventually Judy started going with John. (She didn't meet Neal until she was in college.) John wasn't the only boyfriend she had, but they began gradually to pair off together in the crowd. John was tall, blond, and likeable, and he cared about Judy from the first. Together they laughed a lot and did a lot of fun things, and he spoiled her with gifts and attention. He was crazy about her little sister Loni; when he had to wait for Judy, he spent the time playing with Loni, a happy child with a talent for organizing. John loved the way three-year-old Loni bossed him, and he carried her around on his shoulders and enjoyed playing with her.

It wasn't until a little while before graduation that Judy found out John was not a member of the LDS church. She found out quite by accident, and it upset her so much that she cried for three days.

"I didn't know you cared about John that much," I said.

"I didn't either. But we've had so much fun." Judy shed her tears, and by the next time she went with John, she had made her decision. "I'll go with you to graduation," she told him, "and then that's all. I'll still be your friend but we'll never date again."

"But why?" he asked. "I'm planning to marry you, Judy."

"No. I made up my mind a long time ago that I'd be married in the temple. You don't belong to the Church, and it's hard enough deciding between boys in the Church without starting on the ones who aren't members. I'm going away to college, so that will make it easier."

Judy made her own decision.

Will I always be looking back on Judy's life? I asked myself as the rain splashed on my windshield. *Will I never catch up and be a part of her future, instead of only looking back at the past?* The thought frightened me.

There had been many who had helped Judy, of course. But she always took advantage of her opportunities and put in lots of hard work with every dollar and every chance she had. If there was anything she hadn't put into her life, it was because she hadn't felt the need.

There had been times when I had preached to her, but it was because I wanted her to be aware of dangers that might hurt her. I tried to arm her with the knowledge of her choices and prepare her before she made decisions. Sometimes she complained and said I was the only one who criticized her.

"My friends all think I'm great," she told me. "Why can't I please you, Mother?"

"You do please me," I replied. "But if I don't warn you, if I don't make you aware of your great potential, who will? Your friends haven't the experience to warn you of dangers— they don't love you as much as I do or want as much for you. I want what you want, but I'm more aware of what it takes to earn the things you want in your life. There is a price we pay for everything we get in this life. I don't want you to pay a price that isn't necessary. I'm old enough to see a little further down the road."

After she left, I would feel sorry for having come down on her so hard, but there was a responsibility that went with being the mother of a girl like Judy. I didn't want to fail in following through on that responsibility. How could I ever face myself if I did?

Judy hadn't wasted a minute of her life. As I sat in the audience beside her father and watched her come down the aisle at her high school graduation, I felt as if I had let her down, that perhaps I had missed a lot of her life and accomplishments because my own life was so busy with an active husband and five active children, along with my church callings. I looked closely at the marching seniors and noticed for the first time that a few of them were wearing blue satin trim around their collars. That, according to the program, was for honor students. Then I remembered that Judy had put the trim on before she left home, and I hadn't even known that it was such an important achievement.

Judy had always been on the honor roll through junior high and high school. "It's because of my friends," she said when I teased her about studying so much that she had worn the Formica on her desk smooth. "I have to get good grades because my friends get good grades."

As she took her place on the stage in that lovely auditorium, with the lighted sky-blue backdrop and banks of green shrubbery on each side, I thought how professional everything looked, how well done . . . like Judy.

Don't rush your growing up, Judy, I whispered to myself that graduation night. *Hang back a little and enjoy these years. Stay true so you won't look back with regret. You have so much to give.* The tears flowed all evening and were still in my eyes when she rushed to kiss me and ask the question she always asked after a performance she was part of.

"How was it, Mom?"

"Lovely, like you." She smiled her approval, kissed me again, hugged her father and thanked him for all the money he had furnished for her education. Then she was off to celebrate with her friends.

CHAPTER 5

Judy had gone away to school and stayed with her decision
that it would never be John she would marry. It was difficult. There were times when she was lonely, times when she
missed his spoiling her and laughing with her. There were
times when he came to see her and times when she spent time
with him, trying to maintain her friendship. But John loved
Judy, and that brought her a lot of confusion and heartache.

Judy met Neal while she was attending BYU. Neal was a
University of Utah student. I was appearing in a traveling
musical show, *110 in the Shade*, with his brother, and we
needed another man to sing the part of File. Neal came to
take the part. We practiced in our front room, and often
while we were rehearsing Judy would come home and find us
there. Sometimes some of her boyfriends met her at the front
door, and Neal witnessed that.

When I first met Neal, he had been home from his mission almost two years. He was active at the university and
played football once for the University of Utah Redskins. He
was Young Men's president in my sister's ward, participated

in singing groups, and had plenty of female partners for the activities for which he needed a partner, but he wasn't really going with anyone seriously.

"I'm going to get married in about a year and a half," he told me.

"Oh? Who are you going to marry?"

"I don't know. The person Heavenly Father tells me to marry. In the meantime, I'm not going around kissing girls just for the fun of it. I've got a lot to do."

Judy didn't always have a date when she came home. Some of her boyfriends were on missions, and one was in the service. One Sunday evening when Neal was at our home, Judy made an appearance. Neal left soon after and then called me on the phone to ask if Judy had a date that night.

"I don't know," I said. "I haven't asked her, but she's still here."

Neal hung up, and a few minutes later he called Judy and asked her to go to a fireside with him.

That was the beginning. Neal took her to firesides, wedding receptions, church meetings and activities, and other places that cost little or no money. Her friends laughed at her and asked why she went with that strange missionary who wore his two-year-old missionary suits, drove an old car, and didn't talk much.

"I don't know why I go with him," she would say. "He's fun to be with, and he just comes around when I'm not busy."

In the meantime, John had joined the Church and was now calling Judy for dates. That year for Christmas John gave Judy a ski outfit. And Neal? He gave her a small bottle of cologne, a pair of novelty pantyhose, and a large box of chocolates. His father owned the candy company.

It was Judy's senior year at BYU. Since the school didn't offer a major in dance at that time, she had majored in physical education. She loved her drama classes and participated in almost every play produced at BYU that year. She sang in the chorus, danced, worked on scenery, or helped in some other way. But she didn't get a lead.

"I put in as many hours as the leads do," she complained on the phone, "but I never get a lead."

"Are you showing them what you can do loud and clear?"

"I know, Mom—Peter Pan, but I do try out for every play."

Then one night she called me to tell me she had really made a fool of herself and given her all at a tryout for *The Sound of Music*.

"The director asked me to stay afterwards, Mom. He said he was very impressed with my animation, but that I didn't have the singing range for the music of this show. He wanted to make sure I would try out for the next one." Judy was one of the dancers again.

Then one night she called me and sounded very excited.

"Mom, I tried out for *Bye Bye, Birdie*. It's the traveling musical that is going to tour the European army camps. I didn't think I made it, didn't even bother to look at the call board, but by the end of the day several people told me I was on the list. I went to look, and Mom—I'm in! I don't know what part I have, but they are only taking a few people, so we'll all have good parts."

Later, after her first rehearsal, she called again. "I'm in, Mom! I walked onstage tonight for the first rehearsal and the director said I would be Kim . . . Kim, the teen lead, Mom! It will mean giving up some of my Christmas vacation for rehearsals, but I'm in. We go to Europe for USO camp tours for three months."

It was a triumph for Judy. She worked so hard she lost weight, and since she would only take a few clothes, my job was to put together outfits that were coordinated, that would hold up, and looked smart. The players were given most of the material and would dress alike for their traveling outfits. That meant sewing for me. With Judy's small frame, everything she did meant sewing.

The group was to be an example of good morals and education as well as to entertain the troops overseas. Suddenly Judy's mind was not on boyfriends anymore, but on getting ready to travel, a dream she had had for many years.

In the meantime, John was proposing to Judy every time he went with her. Since he was now a member of the Church, Judy had started dating him again. And Neal? He continued to take her to wedding receptions, firesides, and other church functions, and he was still noncommittal as to how he felt. Judy was beginning to feel it was time to get married. She was grateful she had her show and the trip to Europe to look forward to, so she didn't have to think about getting serious—yet she was serious.

I had one clue one night when she came home from a date with Neal. I was asleep early that night, which didn't often happen. Usually whenever any of the children were out, I spent the time sewing. Milt had a wholesale bakery business and worked nights during the week, so I did a lot of sewing and other work at night. This night he was home and we were both asleep when Judy came in. She crept into our bedroom and awakened me.

"Mom," she said touching my arm softly. Her voice was full of tenderness, and even in the dim light from the hall, I could see that her eyes were full of romance.

"Yes, Judy?"

"Mom, he's so cute."

"He is? You mean Neal?"

"Yes. He kissed me tonight for the first time." She had been going with him about six months.

"He did?"

"Uh-huh." Her eyes were full of stars, shining as if someone had put lights behind them. "He stood me up on the hearth and kissed me." We had a hearth close to the front door, about fifteen inches high. Neal was so much taller than Judy that he often stood her on the hearth so he wouldn't kink his neck from looking down.

"Yes? And?"

"And when he stopped kissing me, I asked him where he had learned to kiss like that. He said, 'Well, Judy, it's been five years since I really kissed a girl.' It was neat, Mom."

As she said good night and slipped out of our bedroom, I put my arm over Milt's chest and whispered, "She'll marry Neal, Milt."

"Now, Shirl," he said, still half-asleep. "Don't start matchmaking."

"I'm just taking my cues from Judy," I said as I snuggled down to go back to sleep.

It took longer than I thought. Neal's year and a half was over, and there were times during the ups and downs of their final decision when I wondered if what I had felt that night was real. The way ahead was not paved with silk.

Neal didn't really want Judy to leave for Europe, but he encouraged her to take the trip because he felt it would be a good opportunity for her. I think she was a little disappointed that he didn't make a fuss and ask her to stay home, but he wasn't a selfish person. We went with her to the airport. Neal spent a few minutes alone with her and was visibly very upset when the director had the students board the plane early. But before she left him, Neal give her his fraternity pin. Judy took it (though I later found out she didn't wear it), and Neal went home to work and wait.

One day I met Neal's brother downtown. I told him Judy needed a summer job, and I wasn't sure where she would get one.

"Oh, she's going to stay home this summer and marry Neal," he told me.

"She is? I didn't know."

"Yes, she is," he said. "Neal's waiting for her."

But Judy's letters, so full of descriptions of the wonderful experiences she was having, didn't reflect that notion. She talked about the conditions under which they had to perform, makeshift stages, sound problems, no dressing rooms. Sometimes the group had to stand in a circle to make a private area where the girls could quickly change clothes. But wherever they went, they were received with great applause and wonderful, spiritual experiences.

"I've received only two letters from Neal," Judy wrote, "and all he says is 'I miss you too.' He writes the dullest letters I've ever read. One thing is sure. I'm not serious about Neal."

When Judy returned home after three months away, her love life began to shape up. Her family and Neal met her at the airport, and after she greeted us all, she went with him. She didn't get home until late, and when she did walk in, I could tell that her vow that Neal was not a contestant was not true.

Judy claimed she wasn't ready to get married, that she needed to find a job. But she talked about marriage a lot. John was back in the picture and constantly asking her to marry him. Neal, however, was still noncommittal.

"Who would you marry, Mother?" she asked me.

"Well, I like both young men. I can't help liking John. And Neal . . . well, from what I've learned from life, I would marry the one who is the most spiritual. Other things come more easily than spirituality."

"I don't know what you mean, Mom." Judy had never given much thought to religious things; they just seemed to come naturally for her. "But I know one thing. I'm smarter than John."

"How do you know that?"

"When John and I argue, I always win because I know more truth than he does. I've been a member of the Church longer. Neal won't argue with me, and if he does take a stand, he always wins because he's been on a mission and knows more than I do."

Then one night she came home from a date and said, "If I marry John, I'll have to take him to church, but if I marry Neal, he'll drag *me*. Neal is strong enough for me to follow; John would just be fun."

Judy spent a lot of time that summer at Bear Lake. That was a challenge for Neal. John had a new boat and was a very good water skier. He could get Judy up on his shoulders and they could ski down the lake. Neal had been on skis only a few times before his mission, but according to Jed, Judy's cousin, Neal was also one of the most coordinated persons Jed had ever known.

It didn't take long for Neal to prove that. He stayed with us at our cabin for a weekend, and before he went home he had advanced enough to have Judy dropping one ski to climb on his shoulders. Neal wasn't afraid of competition.

Finally one morning Judy came to breakfast to tell me about a dream she had had.

"Mom, remember the candlelight ceremonies I told you about at BYU?"

"You mean when a girl gets engaged and shows her ring off to her friends at a candlelight ceremony?"

"Yes. Well, Mom, I dreamed I was getting engaged to Neal and showing off my diamond, and it was so small that I was embarrassed to let any of my friends see it."

Judy was our commercial child, always thinking of quality things, always wanting real gold, big stones, nothing fake. I smiled at her dream.

Then one day she said, "I've been praying a lot, Mom. I'm not really ready to get married yet. I met some of the nicest missionaries in Europe, and some of them said they want to go with me when they come home. After four years in college, I'm still having a wonderful time dating. I don't want to settle down. But I also think Neal is too good to pass up—I don't think he'll wait. So I guess I'll marry him even if all he gives me is a wedding band."

"Has he asked you?"

"No, he hasn't. We talk about marriage and we go to lots of wedding receptions together, but he hasn't asked me. I don't know what kind of game he's playing. He calls me for dates and we have fun, but he hasn't asked me to marry him."

Then one day when Judy came home from a date with Neal, she was very upset. When she pulled out a beautiful ring box, I held my breath. But when she opened it, inside was a carrot—a garden carrot, cut into the shape of a ring, to fit her finger. I laughed.

"It isn't funny," she said. "Do you know what he said?"

"No. What did he say?"

"He said, 'Judy, every time we've gone to a wedding reception and you've looked at the bride's ring, you've always said you wanted a whole karat, so I thought I'd make you one.'"

"That's all?" I was still laughing.

"That's all. And don't laugh. I'm really upset. What do you think, Mother? I just don't know about him."

"I think," I said, smiling, "that my father's old joke is right."

"What old joke?"

"That there are three things you can't hide."

"What three things?"

"Smoke, a man riding on a camel—and love."

Neal didn't call right away after giving Judy the garden carrot ring. He called her father first and asked him out to lunch, and then asked him if he could marry Judy.

"Well," Milt said, more than a little surprised. After all, this was a modern day and age. "Have you asked her?"

"No, sir," said Neal. "I thought I'd ask you first."

"Well, if it's all right with her, it's all right with me."

Milt didn't say anything to Judy, only to me, and I could tell that he was impressed with Neal's attitude. Milt had always been a little old-fashioned, and he was already impressed with Neal's ability to work. To Milt, the workaholic of the world, the answer to everything was work, work, work.

A few days later, Neal called and asked Judy out to dinner, a special, dress-for-dinner kind of date. He took her to a fancy restaurant, where the meal was served in several courses. Judy was delighted. It was their first big dinner date.

Later she told me the details.

It was a lovely, romantic place, with low dinner lights— and very expensive, which impressed Judy. As they finished the meal, including dessert, Neal handed her a Tootsie Roll Pop, her favorite candy sucker. She looked at him in surprise.

"Not in here," she whispered.

"Isn't a Tootsie Roll Pop your favorite?"

"Yes. But not in here."

"Well," he said, looking disappointed, "this is a special kind, one you've never had before."

"All right," she said, reaching for the sucker. As she unraveled the twisted paper, down the stick dropped an engagement ring. The gold band was small, to fit her tiny finger, but the diamond was enormous. Judy gasped and could not believe her eyes. The diamond was a little over a karat, a solitaire. All she could do was smile and give him a giant hug. A little later, looking at her ring, she dared to ask, "Is it real?" Neal nodded.

"Neal," she said at last when she had come to terms with the shock of seeing that much diamond in one place, "if you were going to spoil me with a diamond like this, why were you always so tight on our dates?"

"Well, I am a student and haven't got a lot of money to spend, and I wasn't going to waste it until I knew you were mine," he said triumphantly.

No one ever remembered if Neal asked Judy to marry him, or if she said yes. There was just the ring, and I guess they both knew she would never give up that diamond.

Neal and Judy set their wedding date for September 17. When he learned that Milt's and my anniversary was the same day as his parents' anniversary—September 17—Neal thought it would be special to be married on that date also.

Judy had definite ideas about her wedding. She loved the southern belle atmosphere of *Gone with the Wind*, her favorite movie, so we designed her wedding dress long, with an arc in the front so her ruffled pantaloons would show from the midcalf down. The bridesmaids and the maid of honor wore full-skirt dresses with sashes and had green ruffled pantaloons, and they carried umbrellas decorated with flower centers. I spent most of that summer sewing dresses and pantaloons with miles and miles of ruffles.

Judy had always wanted a small wedding line, with just a maid of honor and two or three bridesmaids. But Neal had five sisters and Judy had three—and they all wanted to participate in the wedding. Every time she thought of having that many bridesmaids, Judy would cry. But when it was finally put together, the wedding line looked beautiful, and Judy was happy she had included all of the sisters.

Neal and Judy were married in the Salt Lake Temple, and the wedding breakfast was held in the Lion House in Salt Lake City. Neal's grandmother furnished a large wedding cake for the bride and groom and two smaller ones for the bride's and the bridegroom's parents. The whole family attended. Judy had three sisters and one brother, Neal had nine brothers and sisters, and our tradition of inviting aunts and uncles made for a very large crowd.

Later that evening, we held a reception in Rosecrest Ward in Salt Lake City. The decorations featured a gazebo in the center of the dance floor, where the wedding presents were displayed. We left the presents wrapped so Judy and Neal could open them together later. The wedding line was on one side of the dance floor, with a southern-style backdrop. What a night that was! So many people came, friends and relatives from far and near.

Neal's little car was parked outside, and the newlyweds ran to it through a shower of rice. But they couldn't get in—the kids had stuffed it full of papers. They pulled out paper while the crowd kept throwing rice, and finally they pulled out enough paper to get in. Neal wasn't really worried, because he planned to take one of his father's cars on the honeymoon. But when they went to exchange cars at an unknown

location, they found the other car stuffed full of papers also.
Friends of Neal had found it.

Later Judy told me they didn't go far that night, just to
the apartment they had fixed up. The next morning they
washed the car and left on their honeymoon at Jackson Hole,
Wyoming.

Now as I drove through the rain, I thought about Judy's
reception and all the presents we put into our cars from that
gazebo. Why was I thinking of the gazebo? It was a small
detail. But life is made up of small details. And sometimes a
lot of small details put together become a crisis, a time of
hurt or of healing. The small things—home, children, family, a wedding. And then illness, a hospital, a crisis. What
did it all mean? All I knew that night was that I couldn't
stand to think about the bad things. I had to focus on the
good times.

Suddenly I found myself on the road leading to Ogden.
In Ogden lived a friend who had given us the herb drink that
had eventually helped calm Judy's nausea and given her added
strength. When nothing else stayed down, the herb drink
did.

In my mind, I was still trying to visualize Judy. It helped
to think about the happy days of her life. She was a happy
person, with a way of making even the difficult times seem
good. Vaguely it registered in my mind that this too was a
good time. Not a happy time, but a time when we were
drawing close as a family, sorting our values, learning to be
supportive and close.

In Ogden I drove to my friend's house. We talked for
quite a while, and it helped to get it all out. My friend encouraged me to continue giving Judy the herbal drink to help her
throw off the temperature.

"That was always what Mother used to do for us when
we were children," I told my friend. "She poured liquids down
us. Mother was a good practical nurse, but in those days I
had never heard of cancer."

"Just keep thinking positive and don't let Judy become discouraged," my friend advised.

"I will. You've made me feel better." I got up and moved toward the door. "I've got to get back. Judy will be upset if I stay away too long. She was afraid she had hurt my feelings when I left so abruptly. I can't let her be upset about anything more than the things she already has to face."

Outside the rain had stopped and there was a clean smell in the air, as if the atmosphere had taken a good shower. *Judy, Judy . . .* Her name ran through my mind as I drove back to Salt Lake City. *Hang on, Judy, hang on. Let's get the job done.*

Soon the turnoff to the hospital was in sight. And soon I would be with Judy again. What had she and Neal and the doctors decided? "Oh, Heavenly Father, don't let her have to have the tubes down her throat," I prayed. Would they dare take the chance and wait?

CHAPTER 6

When I arrived at Judy's room, she reached out for me and I put my arms around her.

"I'm so glad you came back, Mom," she said.

"You can't get rid of me that easy. I was going to go home and let you have a rest from me, but I guess I just can't stay away."

"I need you here, Mom."

"You sound better. You've made a decision." I sat down beside her bed.

"Yes. Neal says we'll wait. Before he left, we had a prayer together, and he said he felt so sure that by morning I would be doing better, and then by afternoon I would start building my own blood, and I'd just get better and better and soon I'd go home."

"Bless Neal. He always prepares himself before he prays and then the answers seem to come to him so clearly."

"I know," Judy said, arranging the extra pillows around her back. "I'm so scared, but I feel good about waiting a little while now."

I moved a chair close to the bed so I could rub Judy's feet. That always seemed to help her relax.

"Vicki called when you were gone," she said, pulling the sheet over her shoulders. "We talked about our decision and how much I rely on Neal."

"What did she say to you, Judy?" I knew that often Judy told Vicki things she didn't discuss with me.

"She said Neal has more to lose than any of us, that he is my priesthood leader and I have a right to trust him."

"And is that the way you feel?"

"Of course. I feel the same way, but it helped to hear her say it."

I told Judy about my friend and how he said taking extra liquids and the herb teas might help her body throw off the infection that was causing the fever. Judy thought about that, and since we knew it couldn't hurt and might help, she started drinking extra liquids.

She slept fitfully, but was up and down drinking and going to the bathroom most of the night. When the nurse checked her temperature, it was going down slowly. Then, toward morning, we both fell asleep and stopped the liquids. The nurse came in to take Judy's temperature again—and it was up. Within minutes the lab technicians were there taking tests.

My heart had a new tightness, a defeated feeling. Now they would certainly start her on the new chemical antibiotic that was still so experimental. It could be very hard on her kidneys.

I said a prayer and tried to keep my feelings from showing. Judy was doing the same thing. *No,* I said to myself. *No, I can't think thoughts like that. I've got to have faith and believe* . . . and even as I said it, I knew I did have faith. I knew she would be all right, that everything would be fine, though I didn't know just how.

"Mom, the new chemical antibiotic could be hard on my kidneys." Judy took my thoughts and put them into words.

"Let's start the liquids again."

"But they've already taken the tests."

"We haven't got the results yet, and the nurse will be in to take your temperature again in a little while."

We went back to the liquids. I made Judy some warm red raspberry leaf tea, one that would be soothing to her empty stomach. As we sat there together, I knew she was praying as hard as I was, even though neither of us said anything about it.

Mid-morning, to our surprise and a new flow of happy tears, Judy's doctor came in with a big smile on his face. No, the temperature wasn't normal yet, but the blood samples they had taken in the night clearly showed that she was making her own blood, much sooner than they expected.

"You'll have some help with that temperature now," her doctor informed us. "And the temperature is coming down."

From that moment on, the news was good. The problems weren't over—there were times of low blood with no energy, and she still had to have some platelets—but the progress was steadily up.

Once during the next few days I tried to explain to Judy that when she got out of the hospital, she would have to take it easy for a while, to rest part of every day, to let herself heal. The effect of my words wasn't good. Her blood count wasn't up that day and she was waiting for platelets. But her reaction took me by surprise.

"But that won't be any kind of living! Why can't I do what I've always done?"

"It's just for a little while. You have to build your strength."

"I don't want to stay in bed to do it."

"Not in bed . . . never mind. I'll be there to help you." I changed the subject quickly. Either I wasn't saying it right, or the idea of changing her life-style, even for a little while, was upsetting her, and I didn't want that.

Neal was with Judy for the weekend. He always brought something to do, making it seem as if they were on a date. This weekend Judy was feeling so much better that Neal invited some friends up to play games for a while. I was at home and had Lyndsy and Derek with me. Judy called me to say all her counts and tests were almost normal and coming up so fast that even the doctor was excited. She would be able to come home Wednesday, five days ahead of schedule.

The news flew as if it had been dropped from an airplane. By the time I arrived at her home early the next morning to get Derek to school on time, a group of her friends in the ward had come in to clean her house. Everything was shining, and even the hall closet was arranged and orderly. There were signs of welcome in and outside the house. I'd made her a banner on my computer, but it looked strangely dull next to the colorful streamers draped around her living room.

When she arrived home on Wednesday, Judy was radiant! Whatever she lacked in actual strength was made up from the adrenaline that flowed from her gratitude and excitement. Her children were so thrilled to have Mom home again that they all wanted to talk at once. And Judy? She looked around her house and the tears mingled with her smiles.

"I'd forgotten how beautiful home is!" she exclaimed.

"Let's get you to bed, Judy," I cautioned. "Don't overdo the first day."

"I won't, Mom. But I'm not going to bed right now. I've been in bed so long, I never want to go there again."

Hard as I tried, there wasn't time for Judy to disappear into her bedroom alone. The phone rang constantly. She did make herself comfortable on one couch or another, but she continued to talk and to look, to smile and to cry tears of happiness.

Judy meant it when she said she didn't ever want to go to bed again. It was only a figure of speech at the time, but it soon turned into a reality. From the minute she came home, she picked up her life again and went on. By the time the day was over, she found that the bed really felt good, but she didn't go back to bed as a patient. She was doing things for and with those she loved—family, friends, and neighbors.

I stayed with her a few days, and we went shopping. I hadn't been shopping with Judy to buy clothes for her since she was in college. What fun we had! Her face was a little thin from her illness, but her figure was still attractive. She was back into size 4 again. We picked out a peach dress, designed with a full skirt and a tiny waist. With her new short wig, she looked like a storybook doll. Her eyes sparkled, and it was hard to get her to go home, even when she realized her strength was being strained.

After she had been home for only a few days, she and Neal flew to California for a party given by her college roommate's husband, as a surprise for his wife's fortieth birthday. They stayed in a hotel, and Judy basked in the warmth of the sun beside the pool, talked, ate good food, visited Disneyland, and felt wonderful. Though I worried about her making the trip so soon after leaving the hospital, when she came home I could see she was rested and her color looked good.

Though she had missed the children, the trip helped her to ease back into her busy life as a wife and the mother of five.

"You've always done so much," I said to Judy as I sat looking at her when she returned. "Promise me one thing, though—that you won't try to repay people for all they have done for you. I know how you like to repay favors and do for others, but this time, just this once, learn how to accept as gracefully as you give. Promise?"

"I promise, Mom. I could never repay everybody. People have been so wonderful to me. Imagine, meals every day for the family, all those days I was in the hospital."

"You have a wonderful Relief Society president and so many friends who want to help," I commented.

And they did. Judy's coming home didn't end the outpourings of concern and help from friends and loved ones. Everyone I met was looking out for Judy and doing things. And Judy? Judy looked wonderful. She wasn't on pills or painkillers or drugs of any kind. In fact, she wasn't in pain. She said she felt better than she had for a long, long time.

Though she was out of the hospital, there were still some decisions that had to be made. If Judy was to go for the cure, the only one available—a bone-marrow transplant, she had to return to the hospital within a month. Even though the chances of becoming completely well weren't very good, if it was to be done it must be while she was still in remission. But going back would mean double the amount of chemotherapy, a few days of radiation treatments, and then going into a sterile bubble. And for a person who had just come through so much, the idea of putting her through any more was unthinkable.

Judy and Neal fasted and prayed before making the decision. Neal was released as bishop, and rescheduled his work at the candy factory to take Fridays and Saturdays off and be able to spend more time with Judy and the children. The Saturday before his release, they made their decision.

"We've decided not to have the transplant, doctor." Judy looked calmly at her doctor, wondering what his reaction would be.

"I can understand that," he said.

"And you aren't mad at me? You'll still be my doctor?"

"Of course. And I'll do all I can to help you. Judy, I've often wondered what decision I would make if I was faced with what you are facing. It would be hard. And I don't think anyone can know the answer to that until they have been in your position."

They were back to normal, together as a family. Within a short time Judy was off with her husband on another trip, this time to a candy manufacturers' convention in Arizona. With snow and cold still dominating the weather in Utah, the Arizona sun presented a strong case.

Four months, four wonderful months. Neal and Judy did everything together. They had been given a second chance, and they were enjoying those blessings. They went on two trips together. And even the cabin, Judy's long-awaited dream of a cabin at Bear Lake for her family, was taking form at last.

"Mom, I could never get Neal enthusiastic about building my cabin, and now, he's taken over and really seems to enjoy the planning and getting it all going," she told me.

"All things come to those who wait." I smiled as I repeated the old cliché.

"Every day counts, Mom. Do you know how wonderful it is to be alive, to feel good and be able to do things?"

And she did it all. It wasn't easy for Judy to admit that she needed help, nor was it easy for her to watch Neal discipline the children when they needed it. He had been a father of quality but never quantity. He made the money—and Judy managed and spent it. When they accomplished one goal, there was always another one to take its place.

While Neal had worked and served as bishop of the ward, Judy had taken care of the house, the children, and her crafts, and had even taught school. Neal hadn't really wanted her to work. She had always taught dance groups, but teaching school was different. He wanted her to be home. However, he also wanted her to be her own person.

And Judy *was* her own person. She always had projects and new ideas to test.

Now Judy had to have some help, and Neal was learning how to do a thousand things he'd never done before. I had watched him take on the role of father and mother while Judy was in the hospital, and I was amazed at how much he could learn in such a short time.

One day as I ironed a few shirts and Judy sat watching a TV show in the basement playroom, we heard some heavy thuds and loud talk from upstairs. Judy listened carefully.

"It's Spencer," she said, pushing the cover off her feet. "I'd better go up. Neal doesn't understand Spencer very well."

"If he doesn't, he will soon."

"Mother, you don't understand. Neal is used to being the good guy all the time. He doesn't discipline the children, especially not Spencer."

"He will now, if you let him."

"He doesn't know how—"

"Judy, I have seen your husband learn a lot of things in these last weeks. I've seen him come in at midnight and look in the refrigerator to see if there was food for breakfast—and if there wasn't, he'd go hunting for an all-night store. Whatever he doesn't know, he will learn. Your husband is a very talented man."

"I know. But I wonder if I can stand it while he learns."

"If you can't stand it, go in your bedroom, shut the door, and turn on the TV until things calm down. You have to learn a few things yourself—especially about resting."

"I know. I do wear out."

"Well, I'm glad to hear you admit it."

We turned the TV up so Judy couldn't hear what was happening upstairs. I had to go get some clothes hangers, and in doing so I passed the hall where Neal was disciplining Spencer. It was all I could do to keep from laughing.

The problem involved something about a pillow, but apparently Spencer hadn't wanted to talk. So Neal was holding him out with one hand while Spencer hit the air. Later, when I was back downstairs ironing and Judy was still watching TV, Neal came down to join us.

"Good thing you're an athlete," I said to break the tension.

"Yeah, and I may have to go back into training." He shook his head. "With Spencer, the problem is to get his attention so we can talk."

I laughed. I liked Spencer. "A cute, normal, energetic, red-blooded American boy—is that what you're saying, Neal?" Neal smiled.

Spencer was a good boy. He had Judy's determination and liked things done well. With Spencer, getting along was a matter of giving him choices, not forcing him. It had taken

Judy a while to learn that about him, and now it seemed it was Neal's turn.

While I stayed with Judy those few days, we spent a lot of time talking, but it was a different kind of talk than the fears we had shared in the hospital. She was working on her journal in the afternoon and read me some of the pages as she reminisced.

"Here's one, Mom. This is when the children were little: 'The children went to bed good tonight. We read our usual story, had prayers, and then sang "Tender Shepherd." We have been singing this every night for almost a year. The kids, Maren and Tucker, love it and sing along sometimes. Then Maren puts her thumb in her mouth and hugs her blanket and goes to sleep. Tucker still sleeps with his blanket and Spencer has a thumb and a blanket.' Mom, do you remember that song from *Peter Pan*?"

"I do. I remember the children wanted me to sing it when they stayed at my house once, but I hadn't learned it and I couldn't find the music."

"Here's another one," Judy said, enjoying going back to when the children were little. "Listen: 'Today I got stuck twice taking Tucker and the other children to preschool. It hasn't stopped snowing since yesterday—we have about two feet now. The kids went outside to play in it and had a great time. I took Spencer and Maren for a ride on the sleigh and Tucker walked. It was so fun to spend time just playing with the children. They love it outside, especially Spencer. I don't let him out very often since he is only nineteen months old.' "

She stopped and looked at me. "Oh, Mom, I need to spend more time with the children. And with Neal." We were both quiet for a few moments. Then she picked up her journal and read some more. "Oh, here's one I remember writing. This one made some changes in me:

" 'Today was the Spiritual Living lesson in Relief Society. We talked about love and living without fear. Then when I got home, after getting the children fed and down for naps, I read the *Ensign*. There was a great article about being a wife and mother. Lately I feel such a need to be a good mother. It's so important to bring up children who have a good self-image and know where they are going in life. There are so many unloved children who are abused or ignored. I want my children to always be loved and feel they are loved.

" 'I went into their rooms tonight and hugged each one as they slept. They are only going to be little once, and I think I had better take more time to love and enjoy them. My projects and self-fulfillment tasks can wait till my kids are older. I'm the type of person who needs outlets, sports, dance, creative projects—but I'm going to try to limit them and spend most of my time and energy in raising fine, responsible, confident children. I also need to be a more loving wife—less selfish. Neal is such a good person and so giving. I'm going to try to take better care of his needs and be a help mate instead of a competitor.' "

"I thought you were all those things, Judy," I said. "You surely know how to play with your children."

"I have taken more time since then. And that's what I want to do now. I've been given another chance at life. I'm going to use it in all the right ways, Mom."

And she did. She and Neal were close, and she kept the children busy and with her, simplifying their schedules so they could all do more things together.

Judy did go on another trip during that time, for a few days with the women of the ward. It was another highlight of her spring. There was one particular incident on that trip that really tickled her. She and her friends were sitting in a fancy restaurant having dinner when two men asked who they were. "Mormon women from Utah," they replied. "We have thirty-one children between us." "Oh," came the return, "we thought you were rich Jewish women from New York."

Judy was delighted with the remark and excited that she and her friends could convey a fashionable image when they were really simply wives and mothers from home.

By the beginning of June, life was back to normal. Summer was just beginning. I was home with Milt again, Vicki was planning her eldest daughter's wedding, the children were out of school, and everyone was looking forward to days ahead at Bear Lake. Neal had been called to serve as an assistant Scoutmaster, and with his two boys as members of the troop, it was a natural calling for him.

Everything seemed normal and wonderful, and we had all started to relax. Loni was coming home to take a dance class at BYU and she would stay a month. She didn't want to be away from her husband, Blaine, of course, but she was ready to admit that, happy as she was, she was homesick. Devro and Lori were also coming for a month and would spend most of the time scuba diving at Bear Lake. And everyone would be home for Monette's wedding on July seventeenth. She was our first grandchild to get married.

It would be a summer of all summers, and I was determined to help keep it that way. Even though Judy was still looking and feeling good, her illness had reminded us that family ties were important, and no one could tell how long we would all be together.

The first week in June I called to see if Judy wanted to ride up to Logan with us that weekend to attend a cousin's wedding reception.

"Great," she replied. "Neal will be on a Scouting trip with the boys, and it will be a good time to get away. I haven't seen my Logan relatives for a long time, especially Grandma."

"I think she'll be there," I said. "At ninety-four, you'd think she couldn't make it, but she does. She is such a fantastic person—and at her age we never know how long she'll be with us."

"You call for me. I'll be ready."

The day of the wedding reception, Milt and I were getting ready to leave to pick up Vicki and Judy when the phone rang. It was Judy.

"What time are you coming, Mother?" she asked.

"We'll be there within the hour," I told her. "Your father wants an early start so he won't be up too late."

"I'm ready. I'll call a baby-sitter."

"All right, see you—"

"Mother?" She cut me off.

"Yes?"

"I went to the doctor for my checkup today." She had been having regular routine checkups and everything had been fine. The doctor had marveled at how well she was doing.

"And how are you this time, dear?"

There was a pause before she answered. "Mother, the cancer cells are back. They showed up in my blood test today."

CHAPTER 7

The old pain was back, starting in my stomach and working up to my heart and filling my throat. How could it be? Judy looked so wonderful and had so much energy—how could it have happened again?

"Oh, Judy . . . you're kidding me," I said over the phone. My mind was telling me what a dumb statement that was— Judy wouldn't kid about her cancer, it was too painful to think about. I just said those words out of habit; they just came out of me while I was falling apart inside.

"I wish I were kidding, Mother. Gayle went with me to the doctor. We were going to go to lunch afterward. She waited a long time, and when I came out she was kind of dozing. I touched her arm and then I heard myself saying, 'I haven't prepared to die. I haven't prepared to die.' I just lost it all, Mom."

"I'm coming up," I said. "I can be there in a few minutes. We won't go to the reception."

"I want to go, Mom. I want to see everybody, especially Grandma."

"But do you feel up to it?" Somehow the conversation went on. Afterward I wondered how we could have talked so calmly.

"Well, I felt just wonderful until the doctor told me. Now I'm beginning to feel tired. Could it all be in my head?"

"Wouldn't that be nice, if it was just all in your head? Judy, are they sure?"

"I have to go in for a bone-marrow test tomorrow. But the doctor says he's sure—he just wants to know more details. They want me in the hospital for chemo in two days, and Neal won't be home by then. He's at Lake Powell with the Scouts. He's somewhere on the trail by now, and I don't know how to get in touch with him."

"Oh, Judy. We'll leave right now. We can talk about it some more when we get there."

"I'll be ready, Mom."

I thought about her words as we drove to meet her. "I'll be ready, Mom." What was in store for her now? Would she be ready if . . . The living images of her last stay in the hospital came clearly into view.

By the time we got to Judy's place, I had told both Vicki and Milt, and we all had our emotions somewhat under control. We decided this was going to be a good night, for Judy's sake.

I ran to the door of her house and she met me. Hugging her like a lost teddy bear, I wondered how she could look so good and be so sick. Nothing showed. She just hugged me and smiled.

As Judy and Vicki hugged each other, Judy asked, "Vicki, do I look like a person who's dying of cancer?"

"No, Judy. They probably have the test mixed up with someone else. You're too suntanned, healthy, and lovely to be dying of cancer."

Judy gave a few instructions to the children and their baby-sitter and then joined us in the car.

"After I talked to you, Mom," she said, as she settled herself in the back seat beside Vicki, "Gayle called."

Dear Gayle, I thought—*always there when Judy needed her, more like a sister than a friend.*

"We never did get our lunch," Judy continued. "After the doctor told me my cancer was back, I was too upset to eat. But right after I got home, after I talked to you, Mom, she called to tell me she knew I needed Neal and that her husband, Reed, would fly his airplane down to Lake Powell to bring him out. It was strange, but when she called the store at the lake, someone remembered seeing Neal and the troop, and they think they can locate him. But it's dark, and they've hiked into a place that's hard to find."

"I hope they find him."

"Reed says he won't come back without him. He's very determined."

"You have so many good friends," I mused. "You have a whole different life here with your friends, a life we as your family don't even know about."

"I know. That's why Neal doesn't ever want to move out of this area. Now, what about tonight? Shall I tell everybody?"

"What do you want to do, Judy?"

"We could wait for the test. No, I don't want everyone feeling sorry for me. I don't think I'll tell them."

"If you don't tell them, they'll assume you are doing great because you look so wonderful."

So that's the way we decided to do it, when we met the family. We wanted to enjoy Judy for now, deeply aware that nothing would ever be the same again, but happy she was with us. But we also needed to talk it out together because it was hurting so much. On the way to Logan we talked about every aspect of the future we could analyze.

"I don't want to go into chemotherapy again," Judy said. "It was too terrible. I'll just take my chances and stay home."

"I don't trust the doctors," Milt said. "They haven't really got a cure. If you go in that hospital, you may never come out."

Vicki agreed. The odds weren't good. We had all been studying the odds ever since the diagnosis in the beginning.

"They haven't got anything else," Judy said. "I can go in for the treatment or stay at home and die there. I think Heavenly Father can heal me at home as well as he can heal me taking chemo."

"We have to do all we can, but . . . "

"But another month in the hospital and trying for remission again. It's harder the second time."

"And then what?"

"If I do get into remission, then four weeks home and then back again. I don't want to do that."

"Can't they let you stay home until you don't feel good and then go in?" Vicki said what we were all thinking.

"I wish they could, but to have a transplant, I have to go in while they are sure the cancer is gone."

"Twice as much chemo and radiation before the bubble?" I tried to make my voice inquiring rather than negative. "And they expect your body to have enough energy left to heal?"

"I know. I can't stand to think of all those chemicals going into my body."

"And the bubble?" Vicki had talked to others who had been in the bubble, and the report was not hopeful. The bubble was a sterilized room where Judy would be alone, where no germs could get to her. I couldn't visualize it; the scene was too terrible to think about. I was glad we were driving into Logan, where at least for a little while we could think about something else. But inwardly I knew that no matter what we said and did that evening, my heart wouldn't be in it.

The reception was beautiful. It was good to see our relatives and friends, and everyone was happy to see Judy, knowing what she had been through. Her ninety-four-year-old grandmother, looking lovely but pale in her pink suit, was teary-eyed as she hugged Judy.

"I've been so worried about you, Judy," she said. "We've got to keep you well. I can't have my grandchildren going before me."

Her logic seemed right, but despite her age, we weren't ready to give *her* up yet either. I had lost my own mother when she was only forty-nine, and even though I felt her influence, it hadn't been easy, and I still missed her.

In spite of fears and heartaches, we laughed a lot that night with our relatives and friends. It was a good time. Milt and I had grown up in Logan, and we found there were still many friends in our old hometown. We came away from the reception feeling rejuvenated. But as we got back into the car to return home, the conversation about Judy's cancer started again. By the time we arrived at her house, she had definitely made up her mind to stay home, enjoy what time she had left with her children and family, and do all she could to try to get well. She felt that she couldn't go on destroying her body with the toxic chemicals, and the radiation frightened her even more.

"What about Monette's wedding, Judy?" Vicki asked.

"Go ahead with it, Vicki. I'll try not to die and spoil it for you. But have it before the transplant, just in case. Any way I stack up the evidence, it doesn't look good. But I have such faith, I know I can be healed. I want Neal to give me a blessing. If Heavenly Father can heal me, why can't he do it at home as well as in the hospital with all those terrible things going into my body?"

I couldn't give her an answer to that because I was feeling the same way. If the chemo hadn't done it the first time, why would the doctors want to try it again? Might the cancer not come back even after Judy was through with the bubble? The bubble and the transplant would involve Devro too. We would have two of our family in the hospital—two lives in jeopardy, because there is always danger when surgery is involved.

Yes, the donor, just as he had predicted, would be Devro. Judy's brother and sisters had all been tested while she was in the hospital the first time. We hadn't talked about the results of the tests because Judy had initially decided against the transplant. Now they would have to be considered.

Vicki and Loni had fainted when the technicians took their blood for testing, while Linda had endured the test. It was frightening for all of them to think of leaving their families and spending that much time in the hospital, but they were willing and ready to give their bone marrow for Judy if she needed it and if theirs was a match. Devro's was the last test. His marrow had matched—the only one that did. Now, if Judy went to the hospital again, he would be the donor.

Vicki's reaction to the results of the test had been, "I am grateful to be the one to care for the children. Heavenly Father must have known I would be best at that."

For Devro to be the donor would mean a trip to Utah from Georgia, putting his business on the line, and keeping his wife and children living out of suitcases for most of the summer. No, I hoped there wouldn't need to be a transplant. But if it did come to that, why not me? Why couldn't I be the donor? Judy answered that question for me: the doctors didn't want old bone marrow. A sibling donor was the only acceptable one.

When we arrived at Judy's, Neal wasn't home from Lake Powell yet, as she had hoped. She called Gayle, who said she expected him about midnight. Any later probably meant Reed couldn't get him out.

Milt took Judy's baby-sitter home. It had been a long and emotional evening, and Judy was showing real signs of exhaustion, so I took her to her bedroom to help her get ready for bed, rub her feet, and talk to her. Vicki straightened the kitchen and cleaned up the mess the children had left.

"The kids know better than that," Judy complained. "They should have cleaned up the kitchen. I told them just before we left." As we walked toward her bedroom, Lyndsy came out to meet her—and to show her how Derek had written on the new wallpaper in the family room.

"Why did you let him do that?" She turned to Derek, her four-year-old, who had also gotten out of bed to greet his mom. "Derek, look what you've done to my pretty paper! Why did you write on it? You're a big boy—you know better than that."

I thought how unimportant the wallpaper was in comparison to the other things on Judy's mind, but not to Judy. She had worked hard to redecorate her home and have everything nice. Writing on the new wallpaper was not a little thing.

"Don't worry about it now, Judy," I said. "Try to relax your mind. You're going to need some sleep before you make decisions."

Vicki, Milt, and I stayed for a while. Milt fell asleep on the couch, and Vicki and I did what we could to straighten the house and make Judy comfortable. But Vicki and Milt both had appointments in the morning, and the hour was late. "Will you be all right until Neal comes?" I asked. I could see she was frightened. "I can take your father and Vicki home and come back." My life, I knew, was on hold as long as Judy needed me.

"I'll be fine. I don't want you driving alone at night."

"Oh, Judy, I do it all the time."

"Besides, I think Neal will be here soon," she said.

"If he doesn't come and you can't sleep, will you please call me?"

"I will, Mom. Maybe I can sleep now. I'm really tired."

"If you don't call tonight, I'll be here in the morning. You won't have to go to the doctor or anything alone."

"I know, Mom." She reached up to give me a hug, and the courageous, tired look in her eyes tied my heart up.

"Oh, Neal, get home soon. Father, let him get home soon," I prayed as we drove away. I wasn't looking forward to trying to sleep, and Judy had even more to think about than I did. She needed Neal's great faith and strength. He could do more for her than any of us could.

"I hope her exhaustion takes over and lets her drift off to sleep," I said to Vicki, who now let her tears flow. "I hate to leave her, but at least she's home and not in the hospital yet."

I called early the next morning. Neal had arrived about three in the morning, and he and Judy had been talking much of the night.

"We're going in for the test this morning," she told me.

"I'll come to stay with the children."

"That'll be great, Mom. I have to know they're safe, and we've got a lot of things to do."

By the time I arrived at Judy's, I had some suggestions to make. Neal had had to leave Spencer and Tucker at Lake Powell with the other Scout leaders, so they wouldn't even know about their mother until the next day. Maren had gone on an outing with the Girl Scouts, leaving only Lyndsy and Derek at home.

"Judy, why don't I take them to Bear Lake with me? Your dad can meet us there. I could handle things there and keep the children happy at the same time. I was going to stay home, but wouldn't that be better? Then you and Neal will be free to do whatever you have to do."

Judy liked the idea, so I packed the children's things. As she helped me, Judy told me how miraculously Reed and another friend had found Neal, and how the trip out of the canyon was another miracle.

The troop had picked up some supplies at the Lake Powell store and started hiking into their first campsite. That was where the storekeeper told the pilot they would be. But when the scouters arrived at the campsite, they decided they had made such good time that they would go on. They were divided in two groups, with Spencer and Tucker in the first one and Neal in the second.

Reed flew over the area where he expected they might be and decided to make the drop to the first group, so it could be passed back to wherever Neal was. He had also arranged for a forest ranger who knew the area to wait with a jeep at one of the only two exits out of the canyon.

The pilot made a run and dropped the note where he thought it would hit the first group. It landed about thirty feet from Neal! The note told Neal that Judy needed him and he was to hike out to the entrance of the canyon, where a jeep would be waiting to take him to the plane.

Neal was tired from hiking all day, but when he got the note, he looked at his new backpack, decided there wasn't anything in it that couldn't be replaced, and dropped it beside the trail. Then, taking only a flashlight and a canteen of water, he was ready to go out. A friend decided to go with him. After a prayer, they started to hike out of the canyon.

"Neal said it was so miraculous, Mom," Judy told me. And I could tell that her faith was reinforced to know that Heavenly Father was watching so closely over them and was aware of their need. "Neal said they seemed to get a burst of new energy, and they walked quickly, with confidence, as if their feet were cushioned with air. The trail and the riverbed seemed to intertwine, spreading out before their flashlights like a ribbon of light, showing them the way."

"I've never had a feeling like that before," said Neal, who had just come into the room. "It was like we were floating, lifted off the ground, and even though we'd hiked all day, we weren't even tired. Several times, when we wondered which way to go, we stopped to pray and the Spirit literally showed us the way. It was as if we were out of ourselves. It was a wonderful feeling."

In the meantime, the ranger was waiting, flashing lights at intervals to guide them. But the wait was long, and finally he told Reed on the shortwave radio, "This is crazy. They'll never make it out of there tonight. We can try again in the morning."

"Wait a little longer," Reed said. "You don't know Neal like I do. He'll come out of there."

Back on the trail, after the two hikers stopped to say another prayer, Neal's friend said, "We're close, within about a mile, but the jeep is above us. We should climb up." They started up, and then they saw the flashing lights.

Within a short time they were at the airport and on their way home.

CHAPTER 8

$\mathbf{N}$eedless to say, this trip to Bear Lake wasn't much fun. There was a deep pain inside me and my throat hurt, but there was a lot to do for the children, and I felt I could help Judy the most by relieving her mind of the worry of them.

Linda called the next morning, Saturday, June 14. I had told her about the return of Judy's cancer and she'd gotten in touch with a friend who worked with a lot of health remedies. But this friend had no comfort or suggestions for Judy's kind of cancer. She told Linda in no uncertain terms that Judy was going to die, that nothing but a priesthood blessing could save her. "This one is a killer," she said, giving examples of people who had tried to fight it with health remedies. She said she always ended up going to their funerals.

We weren't asking for cures, but we had to do all we could. Linda had cried a lot that day and we talked for quite a while. Later I called Judy but I felt that I knew her decision before I called.

"Mom, Neal and I are on our way to see you," she said. "We want to explain everything to you and Daddy. We have made a decision, and we want your help and support. We want you to understand." Inside, I knew she was on her way back to the hospital.

"Judy, I'll support you in any decision you make. You don't have to explain. I'll help you do whatever you decide to do."

"Yes, but we want to explain. We need to talk to you and Dad. Besides, it will be fun to stay overnight at Bear Lake."

"Come on, Judy. We'll be waiting."

Everything in me fought the idea of that hospital. She had been so grateful to get out of there the first time; how could she think of going back again? How could I? I knew Neal didn't understand just how sick she had been because he'd never really been sick in his life. But Judy knew, and if she was going back, there had to be a very good reason.

Milt had arrived the night before, so we had a chance to talk before Judy and Neal arrived. Milt's feelings about hospitals and doctors were worse than mine, so I knew we couldn't depend on him for much comfort.

Judy and Neal arrived late that night. The children were in bed asleep and the cabin was quiet. As I greeted them, there was a new calmness in Judy. Neal was confident, as usual, but I knew he'd been through some soul searching. They sat down and Judy began to tell us what they had been through since I left them. She did most of the talking. Neal watched her and gave her confidence.

"We've had a good day," she said. "It hasn't been easy, but rewarding. Neal gave me a blessing before we went for the test. I had such faith. I felt so strong and so confident that if Neal would just put his hands on my head and say my cancer was gone it would be gone, and I so wanted it gone. I wanted the blessing before we went for the bone-marrow test so the doctors could tell me it wasn't there anymore.

"Neal gave me a beautiful blessing. He blessed the family, the doctors, and all those who would take care of me. He blessed me with strength and courage and all the things I

need except to have it gone. He said that did not come to
him when he blessed me.

"After the blessing we went to the doctor to have the test,
and it showed 95 percent cancer. Then we drove to Ogden to
see our friend with the herb teas that helped me so much
while I was in the hospital last time. Then we went to the
temple. When we got to the temple the last session had already
started, so we went into the chapel to be alone. No one was
in there, and it was a nice place to be quiet and pray." She
paused a moment, reflecting, then went on.

"Mom, I cried and cried and I tried to bargain with the
Lord. I promised I would do anything he wanted me to if he
would just make me better. If I couldn't get better, I still
didn't want to go back to the hospital. I just couldn't. I cried
and prayed and asked . . . and I wasn't getting any answers,
just nothing, like I wasn't even praying.

"Then Neal said maybe I wasn't asking the right questions. So I asked Heavenly Father what He wanted me to do.
And Mom, a wonderful warm feeling came over me. The
answer in my mind was that I should follow my husband,
that he knew and understood and would lead me through. I
could not deny the strength and conviction of that feeling. I
asked Neal what I should do. He said I should take my herb
teas and go for the chemo and the bone-marrow transplant. I
asked him why, and he explained that it had to do with my
preparation and his preparation and the children. It was for
the good of the family and friends and even spilled over into
the ward."

As we sat listening, a calmness came over us, even Milt,
who was so set against doctors and their chemical and antibiotic treatments. He couldn't deny the feeling. Neal repeated
how it had been manifest to him.

Afterwards, Judy said, "So, Mom, I have to go back. It
isn't a matter of whether I'll be cured or not, but a matter of
obedience. Neal said if I decide to stay home and die or take
my chances without the chemo, that is my choice and I will

be on my own. If I go with the answer of chemo and transplant, then Heavenly Father will guide me through."

We talked a long time, and then we all went to bed. The next morning, we got the children up and going and then we just talked. It was a beautiful day, the kind we always dream of for Bear Lake.

Judy went over to the new cabin site to check out the footings and the basic plumbing, and she made some changes in the plan. As we reluctantly walked toward our cars to go home, the children got in their car and Judy and Neal looked around. She looked over the lake, and I could tell from the look in her eyes that she was wondering, with me, if she would ever see it again.

I put my arms around her and said, "Judy, I gave you a lot of orders when you were growing up. Now it's your turn to give me orders. I want you to tell me how I can help you the most. I want to be there for you and to do whatever I can, with your children or in the hospital, wherever I can. I need specific instructions."

She hugged me. "Oh, Mom, I am so frightened. I don't want to do it. I don't want to."

"But your answer was that this is what you have to do?"

She nodded while the tears shone in her eyes.

"Judy," I said, "knowing what I know about that terrible treatment, there isn't anything in this world that would make me go in that hospital. I would take what time I have and stay home—unless . . . unless I had a manifestation the way you did. Whenever you feel frightened or negative, just think of that feeling you had in the temple and have faith in it."

As we drove away, following Judy and Neal and leaving Bear Lake behind, I could see Milt was having a bad time. Bear Lake was Judy. He didn't want to come to Bear Lake without her. He had taught Judy to water-ski when she was twelve years old. He had thrown her a line and told her to hang on. After several tries, he told her he'd leave her out in the water if she didn't hang on. She'd hung on and had become our best skier—a little four-foot-ten girl who could eventually jump off the dock on one ski, whip down the lake in her working uniform, and come back and land on the shore without getting wet. She was her father's Bear Lake girl. I could see the things he had said so often reflected in his teary eyes as we drove away.

Judy had told us, "I want the cabin, Mother, because I want the children to grow up here the way I did, with their cousins around them and you and Dad. I want them to know and love Bear Lake the way I do." She was mentally covering all the bases even though she had said, "Of course I'll come through it and get well, or why would Heavenly Father ask me to do it?"

My thoughts were crazy. The pieces were falling into place, reminding me too much about the way my prayers had been answered so quickly before, as if He were reminding me He was there and in charge and understood. But would the big prayer be answered the way we wanted it answered, or would it be a repeat? I remembered Devro had said, "Yes, it's nice to say you believe in prayer when your prayers are answered the way you want them answered, but what about when the answer is no?" That one kept running through my mind.

I was all right while I was with Judy, but when she and Neal left with the children and Milt and I followed alone in our car, my mind began to dwell on the process ahead. By the time I got home I was thinking deeply about what she was going to do. I knew I would be with her, and I didn't like the odds.

At home I called Loni. As the youngest of our children, I knew she wouldn't take this news easily. But I had to prepare her; I couldn't let her hear from someone else. She would never forgive me for not letting her know if anything happened. When I told her, she cried and asked if Judy was going to die. That was the first time anyone had said it out loud, and it took me off guard. I told her I didn't know, but my voice, I'm sure, wasn't positive enough to be convincing. We cried together. This was the first time I had let myself cry. I'd had a rule about tears ever since my mother was killed: I wouldn't cry until I knew I could stop. Loni had been so torn apart the first time Judy had gone into the hospital and so delighted when she was out, this was a blow she hadn't expected.

"I'm coming home as soon as I can, Mother. Do you care if I don't take that class we'd planned on at BYU and just stay with you for a month? Me and Braden?" Braden was just over a year old, and we were all waiting to see him. "I was going to wait until closer to the wedding, but I want to come soon."

"We'll love having you. What about Blaine?"

"He has a lot of work to do, but maybe he can come the last week for Monette's wedding."

Loni was to be Monette's matron of honor. They had been planning the wedding in the middle of Judy's illness and had thought they had clear days ahead when she would be well. Now we didn't know what would be happening. My niece, too, had gotten engaged—that meant two family weddings before fall. What would the fall bring for Judy? Very bravely Judy had said, the night we went to Logan, "Go ahead with Monette's wedding, Vicki. I'll try not to die and spoil everything." And her smile had been honest while Vicki had struggled to keep from dissolving into tears in front of her.

Later I called Devro. After I told him about Judy, there was a silence. Then I asked him if he was ready for the transplant, ready to give Judy some of his bone marrow.

"You know I will, Mom," he quickly responded. "Lori said, even when Judy decided against it before, that she knew eventually Judy would go through with it. She says she thinks this is as much for me as it is for Judy."

"Dear Lori. What would this family do without her?" I paused, then said, "Dev, it might mean a long stay. What about your business?"

"It'll be all right, Mother." There was suddenly some irritation in his voice. "Mother, you can't prepare people for this, you know?"

"What? I'm not—"

"Mom, whatever happens will be in Judy's hands. It will come from Judy."

I was hurt at first. I wanted to ask him, what did he know? But my thoughts did not turn into words. If anyone knew, Dev did. He had been through it. We had been through it together, and we'd had our negative and our positive feelings before. He was right. I hadn't been as positive as I wanted to be because of this deep feeling inside me.

"I'm sorry, Dev."

"Mother, I learned that you can't prepare people and you can't be negative. We just do all we can to get them well, all we can to help them live."

"I'm trying, Dev—but you're right. Maybe I haven't been positive. I'll do better, Dev. I will, I promise." I swallowed, and the lump in my throat dissolved. "Thanks, Dev. I needed that."

His voice softened. "I don't want to hurt you, Mom."

"What did I say, Dev?"

"It wasn't what you said, Mom. It's in your voice." His tone was gentle now.

I thought about Judy at Bear Lake telling me her decision, and I wondered if my voice had been negative then. I began to worry about that.

"Mom?"

"I'm here, Dev. I'm all right. Thanks, dear. I'm guilty, I know I am. I'll change. I'll change right now and be positive. It isn't that I don't have the faith."

"I know, Mom. But you have influence on so many."

"I know. Thanks, dear."

After hanging up the phone I talked to Milt and he made me feel better. I hadn't said anything wrong at Bear Lake to Judy, but I hadn't given her any dynamic positive attitude, either. I sat down in front of my computer and wrote her a letter.

"Dear Judy, The decision is made. It's full steam ahead. You are in Heavenly Father's hands—who else do you need on your side? We're going for the transplant and you'll make it. You'll get well."

There was a little more to the letter, as I let her know I was available and eager to be her companion and that she could count on my full support. I don't know what the letter did for her, but it helped me.

The next morning, very early, Devro called. I knew he would. No one had more compassion or empathy when he had had time to think about it.

"Mom?"

"Yes, Dev."

"I'm sorry, Mom. I shouldn't have talked to you that way. After all, I've been out here and you've been going through everything alone. Lori reminded me that you were the one sitting beside Judy in the hospital, and I had no right to criticize."

"I needed your words, Dev. I've been feeling sorry for myself. You smacked me—it helped. Thank you. I worried. I hadn't had any manifestation as to where this might take her, except that she will be watched over and guided, and I don't know if it will be for the other side or this one. But I don't need to know."

"I felt terrible all night, just knowing I'd hurt you."

"I knew you'd call. But I depend on you to be open with me. Kiss Lori for me. We'll be all right now. You made me lift up my heavy heart and glue on my smile."

"I love you, Mom. It won't be long now. We're driving out and will stay as long as we need to. We'd planned on the second of July anyway, for the trip to the beaver dams with Dad. Kylee wants to go this year."

The trip to the beaver dams was a tradition with all the boys. Kylee was only four and Milt wasn't sure he could stand the hike, but it gave him something to do to get ready for the trip.

I hurried to get the house in order. I would take some of Judy's children the first day, while Neal was in the hospital with her. Other than that, everything was on hold, except what was absolutely necessary and already scheduled. I had my temple work on Thursdays, which was a good source of strength, and then there was a lot of preparation at home and at Bear Lake for the family: Devro and Lori and their two boys, and Loni and Braden, besides the wedding preparations (I was helping with some of the sewing).

As I worked, I thought about Devro and what he would be going through. He was scared of hospitals. It was no little thing, putting his life on the table. And I couldn't keep the thought away: what if he went through it all and Judy didn't make it?

I had prayed hard not to have it go this far, that she would find another way or stay well. I had learned a lot about what it meant to be a bone-marrow donor. It wouldn't be easy for Devro—a major operation, with over two hundred holes bored into his bones across his back and both hips, and then giving blood every week or sometimes three times a week. No, it wouldn't be easy.

I looked up from my work as Milt came through the back door. I could see he had been having a rough day; there were tears in his eyes. I stood up and put my arms around him.

"It isn't going to be our usual summer of fun at Bear Lake, is it," I said. "We aren't going to have fun this summer at all."

He nodded. He couldn't speak. Milt was a softy about his children.

"But maybe it will be a close summer, with everyone home. That's the best we can hope for: a very close summer."

CHAPTER 9

Judy's second stay in the hospital was different. The chemo didn't make her sick this time. Knowing what to expect, she wasn't as frightened, either. And, of course, it helped not to have a kidney operation and pneumonia as well. She seemed to sail right through the first few days, and suggested I stay with the children, or have them at my place, during this time.

I was sorry that she had to lose her hair again. It was just coming in so curly from the last set of treatments. In a little while she would look like the Tiny Tears doll she had loved so much as a little girl. We laughed about that. Life had become very precious, and she didn't worry about small details.

Judy directed her family's activities and paid the bills from the hospital. By now she had been away from them so much that they were beginning to learn how to get along without her. There were lots of calls every day, and lots of decisions to make, and she made them from her hospital bed. Every morning, noon, and night, four-year-old Derek prayed that his mother would get better and wouldn't die. And Lyndsy never forgot to pray for her mother, no matter whose house she stayed at.

Linda went on with her work as Primary president, tending Derek and Lyndsy along with her own children whenever we needed her. We took turns visiting Judy, and we all prayed like crazy.

Neal, assisted by Dale, Linda's husband, continued to work on the cabin. Judy insisted that Neal spend every minute he could, when he wasn't with her, on the cabin. We were preparing for a family gathering on the 24th of July, when Judy was expected to be out of the hospital and everyone except Blaine would be home.

Vicki and I walked almost every day. We walked for physical and mental therapy. Vicki often felt guilty for feeling healthy when Judy was in the hospital, but life wouldn't stop. We walked and talked about the problems of romance and engagement, love and finances, as they related to Monette's wedding. The wedding had to go on. Vicki's first daughter, our first grandchild to be married—we couldn't let sorrow overcome happiness. My niece Shawna had decided to be married in August, so daily we made decisions about schedules and weddings.

Life was full of one crisis after another, little things and big things, and we tried to go on and be as normal as we could.

Milt bought a convertible. I thought he was crazy at first, but it felt good to drive with him with my hair blowing in the wind and the sun on my head. Driving cleared my mind, and the sun seemed to have a healing effect.

Devro, Lori, and the boys arrived and headed straight for Bear Lake, where I was preparing the cabin. Derek and Lyndsy were with me, and Milt had come for the weekend. Devro and Lori stayed at the lake for a week and talked to Judy on the phone. I knew he wasn't anxious to visit the hospital.

Loni arrived with Braden. When she visited Judy in the hospital, she couldn't believe how wonderful she looked.

Judy's attitude couldn't have been better. "I'm going to get well," she told us. "It's just . . . what do I have to go through to do it?"

Jeddy visited her again, and they spent hours talking about how Heavenly Father loved her and that this illness was not a punishment. Jeddy could comfort Judy in a way no one else could. He could get through to her with his analytic spirituality and with his knowledge of the scriptures and the personality of God.

I had my bad days away from Judy, but had long since turned the decisions over to Heavenly Father completely— asking only, again and again, that she wouldn't suffer more than she absolutely had to. But as I watched her with Neal, a line from her patriarchal blessing, which she had received at age fourteen, rang in my ears: she would counsel with her husband before leaving the earth.

Then came the day when Devro went to visit Judy in the hospital. Lori was with him. They left their boys with Lori's mother and drove to the hospital. Lori waited in the waiting room while he looked around the hospital, where he had spent all those weeks when his first wife was so critically ill. Judy wasn't on the same floor—she was one floor down, but in the same corner. Dev walked around and checked out everything, then went to get Lori. He had been crying.

"Let's go see Judy," he said, and Lori knew he was ready.

They entered the room, and Dev put his arms around Judy, his little sister who was older than he was. They cried together for a few minutes, and then he smiled and told her he was going to give her the reddest bone marrow ever— such good, rich bone marrow that it would probably change her whole personality. From that moment on he didn't cry anymore; he just joked with her, gave her confidence, and cared about her.

Devro and Judy had always been good friends—well, maybe competitors was a better word. He was in elementary school when she went away to college. Judy, always athletic though small, could throw him over her shoulders and bring him down, an act that was very embarrassing to Devro, being the only boy in the family. But he had worked on that, and when she came home from college the first Christmas, he met her in the middle of the living room and flipped her over his shoulders and pinned her.

Judy's boyfriends had always given Devro a bad time. He would brag about what he could do, and then they would take him down. It was sometimes difficult for Dev, but he had weathered it.

"I'm just about as tall as she is," he would say.

"Your ambitions aren't very high, are they," I would tease, referring to Judy's short stature.

From the hospital Judy helped Vicki prepare the wedding invitations. And she also helped Don get Monette's diamond. Judy had bought a diamond from Africa, which Neal was going to have set in a necklace for her for Christmas. She told Don, Monette's fiancé, that she could order him one for a very good price.

One morning Judy called Vicki. "Vicki, tell Don he can buy my diamond. It just arrived, and the one Don wants to order won't be here in time for the wedding."

"But Judy, you've wanted that diamond for such a long time."

"I know. But I can't wear it in the hospital anyway. Don't worry, Vicki. I'm not giving it up because I think I'm going to die. I'll order another one for me."

"Judy, are you sure?"

"I'm sure. I want to do something for Monette—she's tended my children so many times."

Judy was always concerned about her children. Neal had started taking Fridays off as well as Saturdays. Originally he had planned that he would work on the cabin. Now he wanted to spend the time with Judy.

The neighbors had all helped out with her family, but from the first, Judy had worried about her two youngest children. "I just can't have Derek and Lyndsy on their own," she told me. "Neal is wonderful, but he isn't used to being with the children and doesn't know how things go when he's away."

That was when I started keeping Lyndsy with me. Derek was already partly Vicki's. She had always wanted more children, and so Judy had promised to share her baby. She had started leaving Derek with Vicki when he was just tiny, whenever she went on a trip with Neal. Vicki's husband, Richard, drew close to Derek also and loved him like his own son. Vicki had come home recently from a bridal shower to find Derek cuddled in Richard's arms; they were reading stories together.

I thought back to the days when Judy was having her children. She had been married about five years before she had any children, and then she had three in three years.

"Oh, Mother," she said when she found out she was pregnant with Spencer, "do you know what I've said about women who have three children in three years? It was fine to have Tucker, though he was always so active I could hardly keep up. Then when Maren came along the next year and was so good—well, I guess Heavenly Father knew I couldn't handle another Tucker so he sent me Maren. She was a darling. She was always so quiet in her bed and would wait for me whenever I was busy. All she ever needed was her thumb and her blanket."

"I remember that she put her thumb in her mouth from the very first," I said.

"Yes. But now—Now I'm going to have another baby. That's three in three years. I must be crazy. How will I ever take care of another baby?"

"You must have an eager soul up there who just couldn't wait to be part of the family. This baby must have a very important mission and decided you were the parents."

But Neal was delighted. He had always wanted a big family. And, of course, when Spencer arrived, Judy was delighted also. He wasn't as healthy as the first two, but he was eager, and from the first showed he was ready for life.

"He's going to teach you a lot," I said to Judy, watching Spencer wiggling in his bed. "I think he's going to be a worthwhile challenge, and that he was wise enough to get himself here when he wanted to come."

Then Lyndsy had come along. Alive, active, never-sit-still Lyndsy. There was some time between the first three children and Lyndsy, and Judy was able to take more time with her. Lyndsy was always very determined. I told Judy she deserved Lyndsy, because this little girl was just like her mother had been. To me, Lyndsy was Judy all over again.

When Derek was born, he and Judy became good buddies. He called her "Cutie Pie." When the other children were in school, there was just Judy and Derek, enjoying their one-on-one relationship. He was a happy, busy child, intelligent and good at putting puzzles together when he was very little.

Our prayers were answered again, and Judy went into remission for the second time. But, unlike the first time in the hospital, Judy knew that remission was only the beginning. Next came the process of building her blood, the long days of depression when her blood was low and small infections would keep her temperature up. This time the infections didn't go away without the new chemical antibiotic we had avoided earlier. There would be side effects, but what?

The first one was the shakes. After the administration of the drug, Judy would shake and shiver for about forty-five minutes. The first time she shook like that, I was at Bear Lake and Neal was with her. I called her on the phone when she was in the middle of the shakes.

"Don't worry, Mom," she assured me. "It'll go away in a little while." Her voice was shaking so badly I could barely tell what she was saying.

"Shall I come home to be with you tomorrow?" I asked.

"No. Neal's going to the lake to work on the cabin, and my family will need you more than I will. I take the medicine only once a day. Vicki said she'd be with me tomorrow."

That was Judy, always aware of how much others were doing. I wanted to be with her, but I knew Vicki would let me know if there was anything I could do. So I contented myself with phone contact and stayed with the family at Bear Lake a few more days. Then I went home to get ready for the "endowment dinner."

In our family we've had a tradition for those who go through the temple the first time. When the honored person goes through the temple just before his or her wedding, all the married couples of the family get together to give advice and words of wisdom to the bride and groom. I was giving the endowment dinner for Monette and Don.

In the hospital, Judy was doing all she could to get well in time for the wedding. It would be a close race with time, but she wanted to be in the temple when we all met for Monette to get her endowments. Judy pushed the doctor a little, and he allowed her to leave just in time.

The newlyweds-to-be were ready to begin the endowment session, with the family around them, when Judy walked in dressed in white. Everyone cried. Judy was there with all her sisters, her brother, and most of their spouses. Neal couldn't be there; he had gone on a previously scheduled business trip, and Judy would join him after the wedding.

That evening when we gathered in our backyard, we put the advice givers on camera. Derek and Lyndsy were the only children who attended, because they were staying with us. They hugged close to their mother, who looked lovely in her beautiful peach suit and a new wig that looked like her own hair. She didn't look like a forty-year-old woman, but more like the one who might be getting married.

That night, after dinner, when it was Judy's turn to give advice, with tears running down her face she said, "Live every day to its fullest. Be considerate of those you love, because you never know how long you'll have each other."

While the others helped me to clear up and milled around saying good-bye to each other, Judy talked to Jeddy, who had come especially to see her. She was staying with me that night so we could drive to the temple the next morning for the wedding.

After the guests went home we talked a little while I pressed her suit and got her into bed. She was tired, and as she climbed onto the king-size bed, she said, "Mom, Jeddy says if I want to, I can know if I'm going to die or not." Then without waiting for my reply she went on, "I don't want to know."

CHAPTER 10

July 17, Don and Monette's wedding day. Judy and I drove to the temple together for the ceremony. Milt had gone to work earlier and was to meet us there. The ceremony was lovely. Monette, beautiful with her dark complexion and hair, and Don, blond and handsome, so completely in love and happy to have all the details of the wedding resolved, inspired us all as they knelt across the altar and were married for time and all eternity.

Judy smiled and shed a few tears, and I couldn't help thinking how happy she must be that her marriage too was for time and all eternity. No matter what happened in the next few weeks, her marriage would someday be resumed, even if it had to be in another existence.

As a mother, I was happy to know that all five of our children had good, solid, temple marriages. I don't know why that was so comforting at that moment, but it gave me courage.

I was thinking especially about Vicki. After all the hours of strain and work, her dreams for Monette's marriage were a reality. She and her whole family had worked on their yard, their house, their reception—all while Vicki worried about Judy. Now Vicki was crying, but I knew her tears were happy tears—for Monette, but also for Judy.

After the wedding, everyone went outside to have pictures taken on the temple grounds. Judy stayed for a few, and then we drove to the home where the wedding breakfast would be held. Milt had to go back to work, so again Judy and I had the time together.

At the breakfast, Devro teased Judy. When he took a bite of food he called across the table, "Are we eating salad, Judy?" She answered and the conversation turned to the food they would put in their bodies to make sure the match was right for the transplant. As usual, when the family got together there was a lot of talk and a lot of laughs and lots of spirituality. We were close. Our problems and our happiness brought us closer.

Judy was scheduled to leave on a plane, so she wouldn't be at the reception that evening. I knew she'd be better off going to meet Neal, and that she could then rest in a hotel. I went home with her to help her pack. The woman she had hired to care for the children arrived, and Judy gave her some instructions. I had to leave Judy's home early to get back to Richard and Vicki's for the reception. That night we could all relax and enjoy the reception because we didn't have to think about Judy in the hospital. And it was a wonderful evening. People came early and stayed late. Devro and Lori, Linda and Dale had fun taking care of serving the refreshments, which had been prepared by a caterer.

Devro had flown home to Atlanta to take care of business, and arrived back just in time for the wedding and to prepare for the hospital. He had given some blood before he left, so his own would be available if he needed any after the operation. On August 15 he would go in for the operation. Judy would have to be back in the hospital a week before that.

After the wedding, there followed some wonderful days for our family together at Bear Lake. Judy hadn't taken out her Hickman line because it was too painful to put it back in, so she couldn't water-ski, but she put on her bathing suit and had fun driving the boat and running the video camera. With some difficulty, we got her to take naps a few times.

She did look good. She seemed to have plenty of energy and she was cheerful. Toward evening she would become worn out and would be glad to get to bed. But we were all there, even Monette and Don, who pitched a tent and slept on the lawn. We moved the boats out of the garage and filled it with foam mattresses for the children. It was wonderful.

Judy couldn't stay long at Bear Lake because she had to make preparations for returning to the hospital. She wanted to spend some quality time with each of her children. She had considered writing them each a letter, and Lori had even suggested that she have someone videotape her talking to each one, but all there was time for was getting them ready for school and going through personal things in her house. "Just in case," she said. "If anything should happen to me, there are some things I want to go through myself." And since school would start long before she got out of the bubble, she needed to go shopping with each child.

Judy was out of the hospital from July 16 to August 12, a little less than a month. In this time she finished everything she had planned. Each of her sisters spent a day with her to help with her projects. Loni went shopping with her and helped clean out her drawers. Judy told her, "If anything happens to me, I want you to have everything in that dance prop closet. To anyone else it would just be a pile of junk, but you can do wonderful things with it in your dance classes."

I spent a day cleaning, with help from the children. They were really good to do things when Judy was home to instruct.

"It's so hard to let you go back to the hospital when you don't seem sick," Vicki told Judy. "Couldn't you wait until you feel terrible and then go in?"

"I wish I could. It wouldn't be so hard if I didn't feel so good. But for the bone marrow to work, there can't be any sign of cancer, and if I wait too long there might be."

And then Loni got around to asking the question no one else had asked Devro: "Devro, what if you go through all this and she dies anyway?"

Dev was quiet. Then he looked at Loni and said, "I suppose, through prayer, I could find out the end result if I wanted to. But it doesn't matter—I'm going to do it anyway. I don't want to know."

Loni's husband, Blaine, had driven from Washington and stayed a few days. Then it was time for them to go home. Loni had been with us six weeks—the longest she'd ever been separated from Blaine since their wedding—and she was homesick to get back. We had a get-together at Vicki's just before they left. We had a potluck dinner and visited. Then Neal and Judy had to leave to go to a ball game Neal was in charge of. After they left, the rest of us decided to make a tape that she could take to the hospital. Each of us put a message on the tape, which we made not because we thought Judy was going to die, but because we wanted her to have something to listen to when she was in the bubble alone.

Devro talked about competition and the fun times they had had together. Vicki, Linda, and Loni related other experiences and added special messages. Then it was my turn. I wanted to say something helpful but wasn't sure what would give her courage. Then I remembered . . .

"Judy, all of your life, when you lived at home, you insisted that I do things that I didn't feel capable of doing. You would bring me a picture of a dress, or draw a little sketch, and want me to make it for you. I would tell you I couldn't and you'd insist I could. And I did. You made me do it. Now it's my turn. This is going to be the hardest thing you have ever done, but when things get tough, remember, you can do it. You're a fighter, and you can do it. We'll all be in the hospital with you; our hearts and minds will be with you every minute, and our prayers will never stop."

The last weekend Judy was home, after church on Sunday, she and Neal took just their little family of five children to Bear Lake. The rest of us had come home the day before. Judy had to go into the hospital on Tuesday, and she wanted this time with Neal and the children.

They stayed at the lake Sunday night, and Monday they played in the water. Later Maren said she thought it was going to be boring without any cousins, but she said it was great, she didn't have to wait in line for a ski or anything. This would be their last day together. It was a strenuous time, and they didn't get home until late Monday evening. But Judy wasn't worried; she knew she could rest in the hospital.

That Monday I was busy catching up on my work, so I didn't dwell on Judy's going to the hospital the next day. My bad days had been scattered. I hadn't cried much, though the pain was there, in my throat and deep in my stomach. But I had to be positive. I had to trust, believe, and help Judy. And I had to stay well. I couldn't allow myself to get down or I wouldn't be able to see Judy. But it was a very difficult day for Milt. He came home from work Monday morning red-eyed, thinking about Judy. The next day wasn't any better for him. When he came home that morning he was so broken up that I was worried about him.

"I'm not going to give her up," he said with a determined tone in his voice that frightened me. "I'm going to use my priesthood and demand that she stay here. I have been obedient and—"

"Don't you dare do that," I broke in. "We don't want Judy to have to go through any more than necessary just to convince us it's time for her to go or stay. If you hold on to her, you might cause her a lot of extra suffering. Don't do that, Milt. Let's be worthy earthly parents and appreciate what we have of her while she's here and help her with whatever she has to do."

"But she's so young and has so much to live for."

"Milt, would you keep her from a higher calling if she has chosen it?"

"She hasn't chosen it. Judy doesn't want to die."

"We don't know that she will die," I reminded him.

"With all the stuff they put into her, how can she make it through?"

"She has a chance. Heavenly Father will take care of her. I have come to know that this is for some purpose. It is not a punishment. Judy has lived a very obedient and useful life. She has everything to live for. If she doesn't come out of it, then it has to do with her own choosing."

"How do you know that?"

"I have come to know it. I can't deny what I feel. I'm hoping this experience is for her to gain knowledge for this life, but I won't disbelieve if it's not that way. Besides, where do we get off saying we won't give her up? She isn't ours to give. We merely borrowed her; Heavenly Father allowed her to come and stay. We are only earthly parents, after all."

Milt was quiet. Then he said, "If I just trusted the doctors more . . . "

"Milt, they're doing the best they can. I think it's a stupid treatment, to kill everything in your body and then expect it to heal itself. When they find the cure for cancer, it won't be this method, I'm sure of that. But right now this is all there is. They *are* trying. They didn't give her the cancer; they're only doing what they can to save her."

I wasn't telling Milt anything he didn't know. But when I hurt, it always helped me to have someone to talk to, and our discussion seemed to calm Milt.

"Milt, she isn't in the hospital yet," I said. "Why don't we drive to Salt Lake to see her?"

"What good would it do?"

"You could tell her you love her. You haven't told her very often, have you? I think she would love having you drive all the way in to tell her you love her."

So we did. It was a beautiful afternoon, and we drove with the top down on the convertible. When we got to Judy's she wasn't home; she had gone to the store.

Milt had gone into the house to talk to Neal and I was in the front yard when Judy came home. As she jumped out of the car, she was smiling. I told her that her father was feeling bad and had come to see her. She ran past me into her kitchen, where Milt and Neal were talking, and threw her arms around her father.

"You've decided you kinda like me, huh?"

That was it. Her happy disposition broke the ice, and her father hugged her and felt better.

CHAPTER 11

Judy checked into the hospital for the third time on August 12. That weekend I went to Bear Lake with Linda and her children and took Lyndsy and Derek. Before leaving Salt Lake, we stopped at the hospital to see Judy. Neal, Milt, and Linda's husband, Dale, joined us at the lake Friday night. When Neal called Judy Sunday afternoon, she was very weak. The first days of chemo were over, and she was getting ready for the radiation treatment.

We returned from Bear Lake Sunday night, and on Monday I went to see Judy. She looked very pretty in a new nightgown, and she had some beautiful flowers in her room. As we visited, I asked if she would like me to bring in my portable computer so she could learn to use the word processor. She liked the idea. She was getting ready for the bubble isolation now.

After the wedding Dev had had to fly back to Atlanta again to take care of his business. He flew back to Utah on Tuesday, August 19, and spent one night with his family before entering the hospital for the transplant.

The next day, August 20, I spent the morning in the temple. I put Judy and Devro's names on the prayer roll, and I also prayed for answers. Yet, as I came out of the temple that day, the thought came very clearly to my mind: "You foolish mother, you have your answer. Heavenly Father is aware and in charge. You've known that from the beginning. So you are worried about the transplant and wish it didn't have to be—would you deprive your children of the great blessings that this sacrifice will bring?"

Yes, I thought, *it is a good thing mothers aren't given too much power, or we might rob our children of many special difficult blessings.*

That evening we met as a family in the hospital. Devro had been assigned a room just two doors from Judy, and she came to his room so we could all be together. Judy's children came, too. I had never seen Judy looking more radiant than she did that night. She was wearing a pearl-colored satin nightgown, and her makeup made her cheeks look slightly flushed. As the children and her brothers and sisters came in one by one, she hugged each of them.

"This is going to have to last me a long time," she announced as she tightened her arms around Tucker. In the bubble, none of us would be able to touch her without putting on rubber gloves and surgical clothing.

It rained outside that night. The water was coming down so fast that cars were stalling in the streets. Inside the hospital room there wasn't any water except a few tears that came along with the smiles. A closeness and a oneness of purpose filled our hearts, and we had positive feelings of trust and faith.

The children didn't stay long. They were going to visit some of their cousins. They still hadn't seemed to grasp the seriousness of the situation. All they knew, no matter how much we explained, was that their mother was ill in the hospital and she had to stay until she was well. When they saw her, she looked wonderful.

For Derek, there had been a brief moment of realization when she had gone to the hospital the first time. He had gone to preschool that day, but the teacher hadn't seen him enter. She thought he hadn't come yet; then she found him alone in the corner of a side room. She asked him if he wouldn't join the other children, but he wouldn't move out of the corner. Then she questioned him further, and he burst into tears and said his mother was in the hospital and that he didn't think she was ever coming home.

The teacher told him that she too had once been in the hospital, and that she had come home. This had given him some comfort—and then Judy had come home. So the children's faith was constant. To them, that last day before Judy entered the bubble didn't seem really significant. It was just another part of the treatment.

On that evening the excitement of being with their cousins overshadowed the moment of sitting around while adults talked. They stayed long enough for a family prayer and for a hug from their mother. Then Monette and Don took them to their cousins.

In spite of the seriousness of the occasion, we laughed a lot—as usual, with our family. Then we settled down while Milt gave Judy and Devro each a father's blessing. When he finished, he said he knew everything was going to be all right. He felt good about what we were doing. I said, "By that, do you think it means Judy will get well for this life?"

"I do," he said earnestly.

"But you won't base your testimony on that feeling, will you?"

"She'll be all right. They'll both be all right."

"I know," I said.

We didn't stay late. As Lori left Devro and went down to the car with us, she said, "I don't like to leave him alone. I know how frightened he is."

"For a man who has never been sick in his life, but watched others go through such terrible things, he is doing very well," I told her.

"I know," she said. "And I won't worry, because Dev always has help from the other side." Lori's understanding of Dev's relationship with his first wife has always startled me. I have often thought how easy it would be to write a book about Lori. Her example of understanding could save a lot of heartache for those who don't understand. How blessed we are, I thought, that Dev was guided to find our Lori.

By the time I got to the hospital the next morning, Devro was already in surgery and Lori was waiting in his room. Judy was on her way to the bubble. The nurse was spraying disinfectant on the wheelchair she would ride in. I got to see her only a minute, and then she was in the chair being wheeled down to her new room.

Lori and I waited for word from the operating room. Lori had brought her computer to do some work while she waited, but her anxieties wouldn't settle for very long spells. Judy was settled in the bubble and ready for us to see her before Devro came out of the operating room.

In order to see Judy in the bubble, we entered a hall and were each handed a hospital gown, paper shoes, and a cap. Then we went to a scrub basin where we scrubbed our hands, sprayed them with disinfectant, and put on a mask. In those clothes, we could sit beside her bed, just outside the bubble. It was difficult to talk because of the noise of the machinery in the bubble. An air purifier made most of the noise, and I was immediately worried about it blowing on Judy, afraid it might cause pneumonia. Pneumonia and bleeding, rather than the transplant itself, were the cause of death in a high percentage of transplant patients.

While we talked, the first package of bone marrow came from the operating room. The doctor was still taking bone marrow from Devro as they attached this plastic bag to Judy's Hickman line and started it going into her body. It was strange to realize that they took the marrow out of Devro with hypodermic needles and a borer on the end that went inside his bones, but they gave it to Judy through her Hickman line and let it find its own place in her body. The doctor took 850 cc's of bone marrow from Devro, although they had only planned on about 500 cc's. But the doctor said he was pleased and that Devro had come through the operation very well. It was a while before they wheeled him back into his room. We left Judy with Neal and went into Devro's room to be on hand when he came out of the anesthetic. The nurse explained he would remain in the hospital until morning, so his vital signs could be watched closely.

As he opened his eyes and tried to focus them, his first words were, "How's Judy?" Then he slipped back into the fog of anesthetic. A little later, he again asked, "Is Judy all right?"

It was over. Judy and Devro were both on the recovery list and doing as well as could be expected. Devro was determined to get up as soon as his head stopped spinning, and he gave the nurses a bad time when they tried to keep him down. He didn't want the hypo, telling them he was all right, but he did take a painkiller. He was given his own blood back after the operation, and it took a little while for it to run in.

The next evening, we went to the temple with the family for my niece's endowment session. We were to meet afterward at my sister's home for dinner, but first we stopped by to see Devro. We had called Judy, and she was feeling good. She said Devro's blood was really powerful and she was feeling better, so we wanted to see for ourselves how he was doing.

Devro had more soreness than he had anticipated. Lori said he had gotten up that day, dressed, and insisted on going out to find a gift for Judy. He wanted a cuddly animal for her to sleep with because she couldn't have Neal to cuddle. He just wanted to do something for her, he said—as if he hadn't done enough, giving her his bone marrow. The rest of us all felt inadequate beside his gift, yet he wanted her to have even more from him.

Later we joined the family at the dinner for my niece. All of my mother's children and their spouses attended. When the festivities were over, the mother of the bride asked that the brothers and sisters stay so we could have a prayer for Judy and Devro.

It was a beautiful spiritual occasion. We knelt together around my sister's bed, and my eldest brother offered the prayer while the rest of us joined him with tears in our eyes. It was a deeply felt prayer of supplication and faith in our Heavenly Father. We had the family's support. We felt the unity that constitutes strength and purpose. Now what we needed most was Heavenly Father's blessings.

It would be a miracle if Judy were to survive and return to us whole and healthy. I had known that from the beginning. With all the chemicals and medicine being put into her body and with the side effects some of those things produced, I knew that her small, weak body had little chance of surviving.

I had studied nutrition for over thirty years, and I knew the body's functions well enough to realize that our bodies are the scientific wonder of the world. Doctors know a great deal. But no matter how much they know, it would be the body that did the healing, and her body was in the hands of Heavenly Father.

We needed a heavenly miracle, and that was what Judy had asked for: "A little miracle, Neal, just a little miracle. Get me well."

Judy had had many miracles; we had all witnessed them. How many were left? These were my thoughts as I watched Devro get ready for the hospital again, this time to give platelets to Judy. I smiled at my own thoughts. Heavenly Father didn't dole miracles out. He didn't say, "My servant John Doe can have three and Judy four." He was all-powerful, but even He had rules to live by, rules by which He had created the universe. We all have free agency, and we are subject to what we earned before this life and have earned since we came to earth.

Faith to be healed, yes, but what had Judy chosen in the premortal existence, before she came here? What part did I play in her choosing? I have a strong testimony of more than I really understand or could put together scientifically. And now I wondered, even though my faith said that she would be healed, that she would be all right—was the healing for this life or something she had chosen before she came here?

Through prayer, study, and personal manifestations of the Spirit, I know something of the personality of God. He is all knowing. He created the earth and set up the forces by which it functions. There is nothing He doesn't know. I know that within myself.

While God is omniscient and all-knowing, He has told us that we are to live by faith. If we are attuned and have sufficient faith, all things are possible. He is a God of justice for all. He does not favor anyone over another. His laws are just for all.

But God is also merciful. He can intervene with mercy. He also has unconditional love. That is a difficult concept for us—maybe not for God, but for us. We love Heavenly Father when our prayers are being answered in the way we want them to be, but what about when we don't get our own way or when we don't understand the answer?

I wondered what choices Judy had made in her premortal life that governed her life here on earth. What was her mission here on earth? Or was her mission one that meant early death, a completion of her earthly work sooner than the rest of us? Was her mission on the other side so important that she had to leave this existence while her children were still young? I examined my depth of personal knowledge and testimony.

I know that because God is just, He will not break a covenant He has made with someone, if that person keeps the rules and laws of that covenant. Judy was a worthy person. I had watched her through her life. This illness was not a punishment. I felt it had probably come about through natural channels that we did not yet understand. But Judy had always loved and taken care of her body. She had studied nutrition, watched her weight, exercised, and learned to cook right. Oh, if only we knew the answers.

Yes, though we don't have all the answers to life's problems, I know that Heavenly Father can intervene with mercy. Along with my faith that Judy could be healed, I clung to my knowledge of Heavenly Father's quality of mercy. That must have inwardly prompted the prayer so constant in my heart: "Don't let her go through anything she doesn't absolutely have to go through to complete her mission of obedience." That also prompted my making sure the family didn't hold her here with their own will and determination. I wanted to have faith, but not to demand beyond what was best for Judy.

I am grateful for these feelings of trust and faith in the mercy of God. They helped me endure as I watched my valiant daughter fight for life and give herself over to obedience.

Devro, having now experienced a little of hospital life and pain, was more sympathetic with Judy. The first day he was able to get up and walk steadily, he and Lori went in pursuit of the gift they wanted her to have. That afternoon they went to a downtown department store and told the clerk they wanted a big teddy bear and didn't care how much it cost. After some searching, they found just what they were looking for: a white bear, soft and cuddly. The blue ribbon around the neck was slightly shopworn, so Lori looked for a new one. She wanted one in Judy's favorite color.

At last the bear, tied up with the right bow, was ready to meet Judy. Devro gave it to her five days after the transplant, when he returned to the hospital to give the platelets.

This hospital experience was not as successful as we had anticipated. There were problems Devro hadn't been warned of or ever expected to experience. To give platelets, he thought, would be like giving blood. That procedure had been so simple that he had let his two young sons watch as the doctor drew out the blood from his arm with a needle and it flowed through a tube to a bottle. He had talked and explained the procedure to his boys as it happened. It was easy.

Now, as he left for the hospital to give the platelets, he instructed Lori to drop him off at the hospital, go to her mother's to pack their things and get the boys ready to go to the lake, and then pick him up. She followed his instructions, but when she arrived at the hospital, she couldn't find Devro anywhere. She searched and waited, her anxieties increasing. At last Devro appeared—weak, white, and visibly shaken. He also seemed to be very depressed.

Devro had always been such a positive person. When others were down, it was he who built them up. What could have happened to him?

Lori urged him to rest before going to Bear Lake, but Devro insisted on leaving immediately. He was determined to go—with her and the boys, or alone. She took a minute to call me and then followed him to the car.

At home, I worried. What could I do to help? I had hoped he would wait for us or even in Salt Lake until morning.

"Does he know the pump is out at Bear Lake?" I asked Lori. "You won't have any water."

"I know, I told him, but he says he'll buy bottled water. He just wants to get away."

"He's been through so much. I hope you'll be safe. He hates not having his own home here, I know that. But there isn't much help at Bear Lake if he needs a doctor."

"I know. I'm worried, but I don't want to put him through any more problems by opposing him. He doesn't look good, Mom. He's so white."

As she hung up, I fell to my knees and prayed. By the time Milt came home I was ready to get into the car and take off for Bear Lake, even if Devro didn't want me there. My husband stood firm.

"Don't worry, Shirl. He'll be all right."

"But his state of mind—it isn't like Devro."

"He's never been without so much blood. He'll be weak, but he's strong. He'll make it. When he gets there, he'll be so tired he'll fall into bed and sleep. When he wakes up in the morning and finds out the water isn't on, he'll have so many mechanical problems that he won't have time to think about anything else. He'll be just fine."

"But think about Lori, Milt. What will she do if he passes out? She has those two little boys and no help."

"They'll be all right. You offer one of your prayers for Lori."

I leaned on Milt's confidence, added more than just a prayer for Lori, and then went to bed only to wake and pray all night. The next day when I could finally get hold of Lori at the lake, I found out that Milt was right.

While Dev was out working on the pump, Lori told me on the phone what had happened. They had talked all the way to Bear Lake. Mercifully, the boys had slept all the way, leaving the two of them free to talk to each other. I had already learned that Lori is all the medicine Devro needs. She has a way of helping him let go when a situation seems to be beyond control. I've always been grateful for Lori and loved her as a daughter of my own, but never have I felt more grateful for her than at that moment.

To give platelets isn't quite the same as giving blood. It means taking the blood out of one arm, running it through a platelet machine where the red platelets are extracted, and then putting it back in the other arm. The process sometimes takes as long as three hours. Three hours with nothing to do but lie there and think. But in Devro's first experience it was more than lying there thinking.

Supposedly, the doctor had left word that day that Devro was to give platelets. But apparently the word didn't get passed on to the lab. Devro passed the lab on his way to Judy's room and said, "I'm going to see my sister a minute, and then I'll be back to give platelets." This was, after all, a voluntary operation on his part. He hadn't been paid or drafted for it.

He hadn't gone far when a nurse came running after him, calling, "The lab can take you right now."

He smiled and said, "Fine. I'll only be a minute with my sister."

After giving Judy the gift bear, he returned to the lab. As the technician approached, Devro could see that he wasn't in the best of spirits. Dev didn't understand, but he was ready for the procedure. After his arm was sterilized, a technician inserted the needle. Suddenly the pain was excruciating, worse than any pain Dev had ever felt before—not at all like the time he had given blood. When Dev complained, the technician reacted.

"You're a boob," he said. "You haven't got very good veins either. I don't know why you're giving these platelets. I can't find a decent vein to put a needle in. I'm not going to use you again, I can tell you that."

Devro told him how intense the pain was, so he took out the needle and moved it to the other arm. This time the pain was still very intense, but not as bad as before. Dev gritted his teeth and decided he would have to endure it, for Judy's sake. And he did—for almost three hours

The pain of the procedure, the weakness still lingering from his operation, and the technician's surly attitude combined to make Dev quite depressed. Suddenly he was made to feel that the gift he was so willingly giving his sister was creating a problem. We had all understood, to this point, that it was absolutely necessary that Judy receive platelets from the donor, that platelets from others wouldn't work. But the technician had conveyed the idea that he was doing Devro a favor to take his platelets, and that Judy would do better with someone else's.

It was an experience Dev wasn't prepared for. And it took sleep, prayer, and Lori's understanding to calm him down.

The next day, when Judy's nurses heard from Lori what had happened, they said there was no reason for the needle to hurt—that if it hurt, it was because the technician had hit a nerve and should have withdrawn the needle immediately.

They said that giving platelets shouldn't involve any more pain than giving blood.

When he recovered, Devro vowed, "I don't ever want to meet that technician again!"

Suddenly there was an unforeseen complication. When I went to see Judy, she told me she had bad news.

"What is it?" I asked.

"It's probably good news for Devro but bad for me. The platelets didn't take. They didn't do anything for me. Devro's bone marrow was good, and the doctor doesn't think there will be any rejection because we match so well, but the platelets didn't do me any good at all."

"Judy, what does that mean?"

"The doctor hasn't any explanation. He has never known it to happen before. They're giving me platelets from another donor today."

"Don't they want Devro's anymore?"

"The doctor said they'd try once more, but if his platelets aren't compatible, Devro won't have to wait around anymore. He can go home."

"I don't think he'll leave until you're better," I said.

"I don't know what's going to happen, Mother. I can't understand this. And there's something else . . . "

"Yes?"

"I found out that even after a successful transplant, this kind of cancer can come back."

"Oh, Judy!" I could see that she was shaken. I wanted to hug her, but because of the conditions in the bubble, I couldn't touch her, even with my complete surgical clothing on. And all she could see of me, with my mask on, was my eyes. I wondered what was showing there.

"Mother," she explained, "I decided on the transplant even though I was still in remission because I thought I'd be through with the whole thing if I did this . . . but now I know it can come back even with a transplant."

CHAPTER 12

Devro felt terrible that his platelets hadn't helped Judy. He began taking vitamins and trying to beef up his system for a second try. But the following day we got the report that the platelets from another matching donor hadn't worked either. The doctor concluded that the problem was with Judy's system, not the platelets. He prescribed gamma globulin to see if that would build up her system.

When I called Judy, I learned that the gamma globulin was causing some problems. She had a severe pain in her shoulder, where it seemed to have built up, and also a bad sore throat, perhaps from the radiation. Now she had trouble with eating and drinking. Even her herb teas weren't going down, so she had been put on intravenous feedings.

In the meantime, my niece was getting married. I didn't do much to help with the wedding reception, which I would like to have done, but I did go to the wedding breakfast. That evening, after a quick visit to the reception, I took Judy's children to Bear Lake. Vicki would stay the weekend with Judy.

That night, Vicki called and said Judy was having her worst day. Her blood was low, and she was feeling bad about what Devro had been through. She said that she felt she couldn't ask anybody to go through any more for her, especially when the treatments weren't working.

I called Judy. She was crying, and for the first time she had apparently lost confidence.

"Judy, you can't keep Dev or any of us from trying to help you," I said. "You aren't alone in this thing. We're all in the hospital with you in spirit. We're feeling what you are going through, and we're all having a bad time too. If there was just something more we could do . . . it's not being able to do for you that's the hard part. Don't give up now, Judy. It's your low blood talking, making you feel so discouraged. It won't be long now—you'll soon start making your own."

"I hope so, Mom."

"Judy, I wish I could take your place and you could be here with your children. But it doesn't seem to work that way. I love you so dearly; we all love you so much. Judy, I can drive home tonight and be with you. I'm sure the others here can take care of the children. I can be with you in three hours."

"No, there isn't anything you can do. And Vicki will come again in the morning."

"But I don't want you to be alone."

"I'll be all right."

After that, things improved. Devro gave platelets again, and this time Judy's body accepted them, and her count went up. After this, he was scheduled to give them three times a week.

Each time he gave the platelets, Dev went to visit Judy in her bubble. Once when Neal was away, he was there with Vicki and Richard, and Judy asked for a blessing.

"I have to have a painkiller for my throat," she told them. "It hurts so bad. They have two that I can choose from, and I want the one with the least side effects. I need a blessing to be able to make the decision."

So Richard and Devro gave Judy a blessing. Devro told her that she was an eternal lady, and that she had paid the price and all her sins were forgiven.

"I didn't know she had any sins," I said when I heard about the blessing. But I was aware that people often set their standards very high, and maybe Judy was feeling inadequate and needed to know she was doing all right. Dev also told her she could take either painkiller, that it didn't matter which one, because it would be the Savior and His love that would lift her from her bed of affliction.

Judy settled down, made the decision, and for a while that night she had some sleep.

It was now the first of September. When Judy had come home the last time, she had outfitted the children for school. I came back from Bear Lake on Labor Day and stopped at her house to wash the children's clothes and get them ready for school the next day. Derek wasn't going to start pre-school immediately but would stay with Vicki until the woman Judy had hired to care for the children returned from a cruise. For the first week, my sister Ruth, who worked only a few blocks from their home, had offered to come in every day.

We had been held up by heavy traffic and an accident in the canyon, so it was late when we got home. I washed the clothes and waited for Neal, who had stayed behind at Bear Lake to finish up some details so the roof could go on his cabin the next week.

Neal arrived soon after we did, and after unloading the car, he cut the boys' hair. Then he gave each of the children a father's blessing before they started their new year of school. Finally, with the children ready for bed, he called the hospital to find out how Judy was and learned that she was asleep. I drove home late that night.

The next morning when I went to see Judy she had some more news for me. "Mother," she said, "I have pneumonia." Her voice, which had been affected by the illness, was breathy

and quiet. She whispered the words and then waited, looking at me. I stood there in my mask and tried to think of
what to say.

"Mother? I have pneumonia. Doesn't that frighten you?"

I nodded numbly and reached out to put my hands on
her feet. I held them sometimes—they were too sore now to
rub, and I had to be careful that they didn't start bleeding.

"Mother?" She was waiting for my answer, and I could
see the fear in her eyes.

"Yes, Judy," I finally said, "it does frighten me. But all of
this has frightened me from the very beginning. We just have
to remember who is in charge. Long ago it was all taken out
of our hands. Sometimes negative things turn out to be good.
If Heavenly Father can lift you from your bed of affliction,
he can also cure pneumonia."

I stayed until Neal arrived and then went shopping for
some material to make some vests to help cover her lungs
from any drafts in her bubble. I was shaken by how she
looked. She had gained some weight, which meant her kidneys were becoming affected by the illness. There was a little
yellow in her eyes, which worried me. But mostly she was
weak, so weak.

We did have some good news. At the end of two weeks,
the doctor took a bone-marrow test and the results were positive. He let Neal look at the marrow sample under the micro-
scope, and Neal actually saw the new blood cells growing
inside Judy's bones. The marrow had found its place and had
taken root.

"Now can I get excited?" Neal asked Judy when he told
her the news.

Judy later made this entry in her journal: "Neal has been
so positive and always ready to celebrate every good bit of
news. But we aren't through yet; I haven't started making
my own blood or producing white platelets yet."

On Sunday morning I got a call from the hospital from
Judy. I had left Neal with the children late Saturday night,
so I was at my own home.

"Mom . . . " Her voice was raspy and barely audible, but I knew it was Judy.

"Judy? Shall I come?"

"N-no . . . children . . . "

"You want me to go to the children?"

"Y-yes . . . Neal's with me."

"I'm on my way, Judy. I'll leave right now."

I hung up, grabbed my handbag and the keys to the car, and told Milt I was going. I arrived at Judy's to find everything quiet and the shades still down. The front door was locked, so I entered the house through the garage.

Inside I found a note on the table: "Dad, we've gone to church. Spencer didn't feel good. Maybe he's sick or just tired. We locked the doors and let him sleep. Love, Maren."

I went into Spencer's room; he was still asleep. I felt his head. He was a little warm, but I didn't think he had a fever. I got back in the car and went to the ward to pick up the children. On the way I couldn't help comparing this time to the first time Judy had called me.

The children had changed, had grown up, in nine months. They were more independent, and they were learning to take their problems to Neal instead of Judy. That past week Judy had been too ill to make any decisions. One of the last ones she'd had to make was when Lyndsy had called her to ask if she could have a baby kitten the neighbors wanted to give her.

"Lyndsy, I can't have the germs around when I come home," Judy said.

"But I'll take care of it, Mom. Can't I have it?"

"No Lyndsy, you can't. Nobody is home to take care of it. I'm sorry."

Lyndsy had cried. And, after she hung up, Judy, an animal lover herself, had also cried. Her throat was too sore to let any sound come, but the tears rolled down her face. Judy had always been aware of her children's loves and needs, and she didn't like making such decisions. When she went to the hospital the first time, it had upset her to have to get rid of the little puppy that hadn't been house-trained. But Linda had found a buyer for the dog, and that made it easier.

I pulled into the church parking lot and found Lyndsy and Maren. Tucker had gone ahead, and Derek was still staying with Vicki.

"Want a ride home, kids?" I smiled as Lyndsy caught sight of me.

"We walked, Grandma. We can walk home too." Lyndsy loved being independent.

"No, let's ride, Lyndsy," Maren said. "The road is dangerous to cross." Maren had taken over the role of mother and had become aware of dangers.

As we drove home, we talked about what we would fix for dinner.

"I can take you to my place or just help you fix dinner here," I said.

"I can make a dessert," Maren spoke up. "I always make the dessert for family home evening."

"Let's cook here then. Your father will probably be home in time for family home evening." I knew that Judy's family held their home evening on Sunday afternoon.

"Dad went up to see Mom in the night," Maren told me.

"Is she a lot worse?"

"I don't know. He just told us he was going to the hospital."

I put chicken and potatoes on the stove and then called the nurse so I wouldn't disturb Judy if she was resting. I told the nurse who I was and asked for a report.

"She couldn't breathe very well in the night and couldn't swallow anything," she said. "She had us call Neal and he came. He looked down her throat and had us call in a specialist. They took some clogs out of her throat, so she's resting easier now."

I waited with the children until Neal came home. He explained that when he looked down Judy's throat, it looked as if the whole lining of her mouth was coming out. The specialist who came found that oozing blood had hardened, and so he took it out. After that she could rest, but she hadn't been able to swallow even any liquids. She was very weak.

Neal held family home evening with the children and then wanted to take them to see Judy, but when he called the hospital, Judy said she didn't want them to come. That wasn't like Judy. Later, Linda and Lori came to bring Derek home, since the woman Judy had engaged was back from her cruise and ready to come and take care of the children. That meant Derek could go to preschool. Linda and Lori wanted to go to the hospital to see Judy, but again, when we called the nurse, she said Judy had requested no visitors that night.

Monday morning I got in the convertible and drove to the hospital. A storm was brewing, with the wind blowing debris across the road and the sky becoming black. I thought about putting up the top of the convertible, but the wind felt good to me. I drove faster, trying to outrun the storm. As I drove, tears stung my eyes, but I hurt too much to cry. I prayed, pleading with the Lord.

"Heavenly Father, why does she have to be so sick? It's been ten days now that she has been going through this. She's so good, so worthy—and she's fighting so hard to live for her husband and children. Help her, help her, make her well or take her, don't let her struggle on and on . . . I want what is best for Judy but now, Heavenly Father—please be aware of her."

I knew that Heavenly Father was now the only one who could help Judy. The doctors had done everything they could, had given her everything they had. And the transplant was working. So why wasn't she getting better?

I entered Judy's room, dressed in my surgical clothing, and then went into the bubble. As I stopped at the foot of her bed, she looked up and I knew she was glad I was there.

"I'm moving in, Judy," I said, "and I'm not leaving until you're well."

Her eyes showed her gratitude and she whispered her thanks. It was difficult for her to talk. It was also difficult for her to breathe, and when the doctor came in, he ordered oxygen with a vapor of water to ease her effort in breathing. She wouldn't let the technician put the apparatus on her face— it was too confining—so I helped her hold it. Her head was raised so that she wouldn't choke from the drip in her throat. On her head was a peach-colored scarf, and she still wore her big loop gold earrings and had five rings on her fingers. She had taken off her gold chains and put on the hospital gowns. I had brought the vests I made for her, but they were still being sterilized.

I spent the day with Judy inside the bubble, telling her about the children, gently caressing her feet where they burned and rubbing her shoulders, and sitting quietly in the rocking chair beside her bed when she dozed off.

The hissing of the water in the oxygen machine bothered her. There were too many machine noises in the room. When she asked the nurse if she could turn the machine off for a while, the nurse said the technician had to turn it off. Judy endured the noise for a while and then pulled her sheet off her bed and threw it around the machine. She was my Judy to the end—getting things done one way or another.

We ordered herb tea but she couldn't swallow much of it. She was tired of the bed, but she didn't have the strength to sit up for very long. I felt so helpless, so useless. All I could do was sit and watch Judy go through this test of illness.

"Come on, Judy," I said. "Let's teach your body how to relax. No matter what's happening to you, it will be better if you can relax." So we started with her feet. "Feel them heavy, with no tightness, just hanging limp . . . and then your thighs . . . now your stomach muscles . . . your chest . . . " And so on up her body, as she tried to breathe deep and let her body hang heavy. When we finished she would say, "Do it again."

I was aware, even though I felt useless, that these were precious moments together, moments when I could share with her some of her trials just as I had shared her triumphs. I was glad to be there even though it hurt.

On Tuesday morning, September 9, I could see that Judy was getting worse. She had been given the chemical antibiotic that had made her shake earlier, but this time she had no reaction to it. Also the whites of her eyes were now more yellow. Her responses were slower; she would sit in one position longer, a little dazed. I didn't want to leave her at all. When the doctor came to see her, she could talk only in a whisper. He asked how she was feeling and if she was in any pain. She shook her head but touched her left side and said she had a strange little feeling there.

"An ache or a pain?" To examine her, the doctor had to put his hands into the plastic gloves that were part of the screen around the bubble.

"Just funny, kind of an ache," she whispered in my ear so I could tell the doctor.

"No other pain?"

Judy shook her head.

After the doctor left, the nurses told her she had to have her body gases taken. That frightened her. She had had that done once before, and it had been very painful.

When the special nurse came to take body gases, Judy reached for my hand and squeezed it tight.

"Just look at me, not at what they are doing," I said. She looked at me and mentally prepared for the pain, but it was over before she felt anything. She was very relieved.

Vicki came up to see her, stopping by on her way home from work. Judy hadn't wanted any visitors for a long time, but when Vicki came she smiled and indicated the chair beside her.

"I won't come inside the bubble, Judy, and I don't want to tire you," Vicki said. "I just wanted to see you." She stood outside the bubble, and I brought her a chair. Judy seemed delighted to see her and said, loud enough for Vicki to hear above all the noise, "Now sit right there and tell me the news."

While Vicki told Judy about some of the things Derek was doing and saying, and about the other children, I went out in the hall to take a break. Afterwards Judy got up to sit in the rocking chair, and I sat in the chair outside the bubble so I could run the TV. *Winds of War*, a miniseries, was coming on, and Judy said she wanted to see it. We were waiting for it to start when the doctor came in for the second time that evening. He checked her charts and her, then stood looking at her. Judy pulled my head down to whisper in my ear the questions she wanted me to ask him. They had a good relationship, and he was always direct in answering her questions.

"Am I doing all right, doctor?"

"No, Judy, you aren't doing very well."

"Are you worried about me?"

"Yes, Judy, I am, but then, I'm a worrier."

"Am I doing as well as other transplants?"

"Not as well as some."

When he left, I watched a cloud of darkness cross Judy's face. "Mom, he's worried about me," she whispered.

"He says your white platelets should be building by Thursday," I reminded her, "and that will change things. Hold on."

Suddenly Judy sat up and reached for a paper beside her bed. When I started to say something she shushed me, and I realized she was reading the transcript of a blessing Neal had given her. Then she handed the paper to me and lay back in her bed. I read the paper. It was a beautiful blessing, but it didn't indicate if the blessings were for this life or for the life hereafter. I reached for her hand and she held my hand tightly; for a few minutes, her eyes shut. Finally she opened her eyes, reached up to pull me down to her, and said she wanted me to sit down because I had been standing too long. With all she was going through, she was still thinking of me.

To watch the television, I moved out of the bubble again so she could sit in the rocking chair. She was restless and kept shifting into different positions to relieve her tired back. She was a little chilly, so she kept the bedspread around her back even when she sat up. She still had her little peach-colored hat on.

After *Winds of War*, she slept a little, but kept waking up. Sitting up, she moved her hand around her head. "That war picture, it's making me crazy," she said. "I'm thinking funny things."

"We shouldn't have watched it. Shall we put on a movie?"

She nodded, and I stepped out of the bubble to run the VCR machine. I didn't leave the bubble often because it meant I had to go through the sterilization process again before I could return, and if she needed me, that would take too much time.

"We have *Heaven Can Wait*," I said. "That's a fun movie. Want to see it?" She nodded, and I put it on the video.

As we watched the movie we both tried to get our minds off her illness. She smiled at some of the funny scenes, and I laughed where I could. Just before it was over, at two in the morning, she climbed back into bed. The nurse wanted to take her temperature so I turned the show off for a minute, but Judy whispered as loud as she could, "No, let's finish it."

We did finish it while the nurse checked her. Judy's breathing was very fast and she was chilling. I put on my surgical clothes again and went into the bubble, piled some pillows on her feet, and covered her up, tucking her in. I held the oxygen for her to breathe. Then suddenly she wasn't chilling anymore but burning up. I called the nurse for ice packs for her feet and head.

As I was holding the ice pack on her head, and the oxygen too, Judy pulled my head down and whispered in my ear, "Call Neal. Tell him not to shower or shave, but *come*."

I reached over to pick up the phone. Neal answered, groggy with sleep, and I gave him the message, then went on with the ice treatment.

When Neal arrived, he dressed in his surgical clothing and came right in. The first thing he did was to give Judy a blessing. In it he told her that her body would respond immediately to the medication, that the healing process would begin immediately, and that she would be made completely well, with no side effects.

Because it was so crowded in the bubble, I told Neal I would rest on the bed outside the bubble until he was ready to go to work. The blessing had made me feel better, and as I lay down on the bed, for the first time in several nights I fell into a deep sleep. It was about five in the morning.

I don't know what awakened me, but suddenly I sat straight up. How could I have fallen asleep when Judy was so ill? I had slept about two hours. Jumping up, I went around the curtain. To my surprise, Neal was not sitting in the rocking chair dozing as he usually did. He was standing over Judy and seemed very nervous. She looked strange to me—quiet but not sleeping, and still breathing rapidly. I asked how she was.

"She's a little out of her head," Neal said. "She's been saying some funny things."

"What kind of things?"

"She asked me who all these people in the room were."

"And what did you say?"

"I told her there were only the two of us. But then she said, 'It's so noisy I can't sleep. Who are all these people?' "

"Neal, I don't think she's out of her head. I think there are messengers here with her." He looked at me unbelievingly. "Neal, with all the praying I've been doing . . . I've been talking to Mother in my mind all day."

Neal turned back to her and I went to a phone to call Milt, who was at work.

"She isn't doing well, Milt," I said. "It looks bad."

"I figured that, when you didn't come home for two nights," he said. "I can't stand thinking about it. There isn't anything I can do and I can't think here at my desk, so I'm going out to do some physical work." When he said that, I knew how worried he was. He had never been comfortable around illness; his way of dealing with this was to try to work it out.

I went back to check on Judy. Neal was helping her get up to go to the bathroom, but she could hardly make it, even to the chair beside her bed. He picked her up.

I turned to talk to the nurse. "She's very ill, isn't she."

The nurse looked at me directly and nodded.

"Have you ever seen anyone else this sick get better?"

"Well, there was one lady, but it took a long time."

I went to the phone again and called home. I knew Devro was coming to the hospital that day to give platelets. When no one answered at my place, I called Linda and asked if she knew where Dev and Lori were.

"Yes, Mom, they're on their way here. I'm going to tend the boys for them while they go to the hospital. They should be here any minute."

"Linda, tell them to check in Judy's room before Dev gives platelets."

"Mom, how bad is she?"

"She's very bad, Linda." I was careful with my words because I felt that sometimes I had been an alarmist, and I didn't want to be overly negative.

"Mom, is she going to . . . "

"I don't know, Linda."

"Mom, I want to see her."

"Are you sure? Are you sure you want to see her like this, or to remember—"

"I want to see her, no matter how she looks. Shall I come now?" I hesitated, then asked her to wait while I asked the nurse. The nurse told me, "Yes, if she wants to be sure of seeing Judy, she should come this morning." The way she said it, I felt that the time could be close.

I gave Linda the message, then returned to Judy and Neal. I noticed that she had been sitting a long time, as if she couldn't move. I heard Neal ask her, "Judy, Judy, do you want me to lift you back in bed?" As I watched him pick her up and put her in bed, her eyes rolled back in her head and she stopped breathing. Neal commanded her in the name of Jesus Christ to come back, and she started breathing again.

Since Neal was with her, I went out in the hall to get a drink. I stopped to talk to one of Judy's nurses, a woman who had been with her from the beginning and who knew the case well.

"She's very bad, I know," I said. "When they get to this point, does it last long?"

"Sometimes. But the doctor hasn't ordered intensive care or anything like that. He's never had anyone come out of intensive care with this kind of cancer. He'll leave her right where she is, in that room, until she's well."

"But don't you know how long it might take?"

"If she can hang on until tomorrow, and if she can build white platelets, she'll have a chance."

I went back and stood by the door of the bubble. Judy was lying quietly now, though her breathing was short and still fast. Neal said, "She's so tired. I'm not going to let them disturb her anymore until she's had some sleep."

Devro and Lori arrived, and I met them at the door. "Dev, she's so bad . . . "

"Mom, she's going to be all right. I'm going up to give her some platelets now. She'll be all right."

He was nervous, but I knew he wasn't ready to hear anything I could tell him. He walked over to the door of the bubble and spoke to her.

"Judy, I'm here to give you some platelets."

She didn't move.

Neal looked at Devro and said, "She's really tired."

"I know. The platelets will give her strength." The nurses were already preparing to give Judy blood.

"How do you feel, Devro?"

"I feel great, Neal. Never better." The day before, it had taken him all day to recover from the last platelets he had given. He was getting low on blood. But he was enthusiastic.

"I've got lots of platelets. I can give her blood, too." He asked the nurse, "Don't you want some live blood?" She shook her head. "Well, how about white platelets, then? I could give her some white platelets."

"No," she said, "they would give her too much liquid." The blood plasma had just arrived, and the medical personnel started giving it to her.

"All right, Neal," Devro said, "I'll go up and give the platelets. I'll be right back."

"Yes, Devro. That should make her feel a lot better."

They were like a couple of kids plotting. I kept looking at the door, hoping Linda would be there soon. Lori told me she and Devro hadn't left their children with her but had made other arrangements so she could come to the hospital. I wasn't sure how much time Judy had left, and I kept praying Linda would make it—but I also prayed that Judy wouldn't have to suffer more than necessary unless she could get better. My prayer was like a broken record, going on and on in my mind.

Reed and Gayle, Neal and Judy's good friends, came to the door, so I dressed and went into the bubble to be with Judy while Neal talked to them in the hall. As I entered, I held the oxygen for Judy and said, "Judy, I'm still here. It's Mom, Judy." I had a feeling she heard me. I sensed that she had heard Devro too, but was just too tired to open her eyes.

The oxygen bottle was out of water, so I laid it on her pillow and moved around the bed to get the filler from the table. Then I stood beside her again to hold the oxygen to her nose. She seemed to be breathing slower. I moved her head slightly, to see if lifting her chin wouldn't help her breathing a little. As I moved her, there was a little gurgle in her throat. I looked up and saw Linda come in.

"Linda!" I called over the sound of the equipment. "Come in here!" I motioned to her to come fast. "Don't worry about dressing, just come. And tell Neal!"

Judy was taking slow, long breaths, and I knew she was going. Linda came in quickly and leaned across the bed and touched her hand. Judy took two more long breaths and stopped.

My cries to Linda had put the nurses and an intern in motion. Neal also came in quickly and I moved aside while he leaned over Judy and called her name.

"Judy . . . Judy . . . " He shook her shoulders a little. I heard the doctor say he couldn't get a heartbeat. "Do something—do something," Neal demanded.

"What do you want us to do?" the nurse said.

"Make her breathe. She can't live if she can't breathe."

"Neal," I said gently. He looked up with a desperate expression in his eyes. "Neal . . . her heart's stopped beating. Let her go quietly."

Neal moved back as if I had hit him in the stomach with a baseball bat, and he looked desperate and unbelieving. The nurses and doctor left. I put my arms around Linda, and we moved to the doorway of the bubble.

Then someone pulled the curtain that covered the window of the bubble and I heard Neal say, "Oh, Judy, Judy, I love you so much . . . "

CHAPTER 13

Linda, Devro is still up giving platelets!"

"Yes, and Vicki is on her way here."

I couldn't quite read the look in Linda's eyes, but I knew we were both thinking how hard it would be for Vicki. "We'd better go tell Dev, Mom." Linda sniffed back her tears while I made a quick call to Milt's office and asked the secretary to have him get in touch with me. I didn't want anyone else to tell him. Then Linda and I went to find Devro and Lori.

Lori was standing at the door to the lab, and we could hear Devro talking as we approached. Lori turned to us, and I nodded. She got the message and burst into tears. "No, no . . . I don't know what this will do to Dev," she said.

A nurse had called from Judy's room to let the technician know that there wouldn't be a need for any more platelets, so the technician was taking the tubes out of Devro when we got there. He got off the table and came out in the hall to meet us. He was shaking his head a little and his mouth was a tight line, but what I didn't know was that he still didn't realize what had happened. He came toward us and asked, "How is she, Mom?"

I stopped. "Devro . . . she's gone."

His mouth dropped open and something inside him seemed to erupt. "No! No! No!" Those words started the deepest, most soul-rending cry I have ever heard. He cried and cried, with his arms around Lori, and somehow we all made our way back to the room where Judy was. As we approached I could hear Neal's sobs, and Devro made his way through the door and behind the curtain to be with him.

In the hall, I met Reed and Gayle, who had been through it all with us. When I told them about Judy, they both broke down. I put my arms around Reed and said, "You've done so much and have been such a good friend." He went in—as usual, he wanted to be beside Neal. Gayle stayed outside while she struggled to control her emotions.

Inside again, Milt called and I told him. He said he wanted to be with us and left his tools on the job and was on his way.

Next I called Loni. When she answered I asked if she was alone. She told me her Primary president was with her.

"That's good. I didn't want you alone."

"Mom, what is it? Is Judy worse?"

"Loni, Judy is gone."

"Mom, I don't believe it." Then all I heard for a minute were her sobs. "B-but Mom, she looked so good. Why didn't you let us know?"

"It happened fast, before we realized. We're very blessed, Loni. She could have suffered so much more."

"I want to come . . . we'll come. Blaine'll be home soon and we're coming."

Devro was still having a bad time. Though he had comforted Neal, he was now falling apart again, and I worried that he might pass out. He was much weaker than he realized.

The door opened and Vicki came in. Linda met her, and from the look on Linda's face, even before she saw the others, she knew. Everyone was crying and Neal was holding Judy's hand. Lori went over to Vicki and put her arms around her. "I'm so sorry, Vicki," she said.

Devro put his arms around Vicki too, and they both cried, holding each other, each one worried about the other. Then Neal reached for Vicki and hugged her.

Milt came, and Devro and Lori went down the hall to meet him, getting there before I did. It was hard on Milt. He had known what was going to happen, inside he had known, and I knew he knew.

More of Neal's and Judy's friends arrived, friends who had cleaned her house, visited, stayed close to her through the years and through her illness. They were all upset but soon found control and started to help Neal put together an obituary for the paper.

I called the candy company and told Neal's brother the news, and suddenly people came from everywhere.

I took Judy's gold earrings out of her ears and the nurse came to help take off her rings: the big diamond Neal had given her, which she had worn to the end, along with gold rings on three other fingers. Judy's little hat was still on her head, and at last she looked like she was really asleep and not struggling to breathe.

"I guess it's a good thing you were with her when she stopped breathing," Neal said to me. "I might have tried to call her back again. I guess she needed to go, and you made her passing easy."

"Did you know, Neal, ever?"

"I knew this morning when you called me. Before I left home I had a prayer and asked the direct question. I really got the answer that she was dying, but I didn't want to believe it. Even now, when she died, I turned and put my hands on her head and had every intention of calling her back, but something inside me wouldn't let me." He took a deep breath. "I'm going home to get the children. I want them to see her here where she died."

The nurses straightened up the bubble, pulling back the plastic that separated it from the outer room, and took the clutter of machinery and some of the equipment out of the room. The machinery and the air purifier were all turned off now—it was an ordinary, quiet hospital room. The nurse straightened Judy's bed and Neal went home to get the children

It was afternoon when they came back. The curtains on the west side of Judy's bed were open and the sun came in, falling on her as she lay in the bed. Beside the bed was a bouquet of her favorite flowers, silk talisman roses, put there by Devro. We all moved back, overcome by the peacefulness and simple beauty of the scene, and spoke in softer tones as we waited for the children. Later I found out what had been happening at home.

The children were picked up at their schools by family friends. When they got home, they were curious and immediately started asking questions. Neal gathered them together and had them sit down. Not finding the words to break the news easily, he blurted out, "Judy's dead . . . "

He spent some time with the children and evidently was able to give them some good counsel. They all cried except Spencer, who was apparently angry and felt cheated—he asked who was going to help him with his homework and seemed confused.

When the children and Neal arrived at the hospital, we all stood on the other side of the room and the children filed in to stand beside the bed and to sit in the chairs beside it. They all cried. I stepped forward and put my arms around them one at a time, and they moved from me to their other grandmother and grandfather and the family.

"Your mother can always watch over you now, be with you and not be sick anymore. You just won't see her, but she'll be there if you need her," I told them.

Maren nodded, and the others seemed to understand too. I was aware of the shock they were going through and I so wanted to take it from them, but this was a problem they had to work out, their fight and test, and no matter how much the rest of us wanted to help, there would be certain things they just had to do for themselves.

We packed up Judy's things and left the room, leaving Neal alone with her once more. I told him we would meet him at his home later.

That evening Devro and Lori met me at Neal's place, and I put my arms around Devro.

"You hugged everyone but me," I said. "Do I get mine now?" Devro put his arms around me and I felt his body heave. Then I looked at him again. "I think you washed away a hundred years of emotion today, Dev."

"I think I did, Mom. I think I did."

"Thank heaven for Lori," I commented. "How blessed you—and we—are to have her."

"I wonder if there's another Lori somewhere out there," Neal said quietly, and I knew that in the midst of all the hurt, he was getting a vision of how hard life was going to be without Judy.

Vicki had remained behind earlier to help Neal make arrangements after he left the hospital. She said that as they drove around he had said, "Vicki, life with Judy has been so exciting that I don't know if it's going to be worth living without her."

"I know, Neal," she said, "but you have children who are part of her. You'll have to make it worth living for them."

"That's right. I have the children."

Milt and I stayed at Neal's place late that evening, visiting and comforting those who came to call. Comforting others looking at the blessings and the positive things, helped comfort me.

The next morning I felt wrung out. I called Linda and she felt the same way. We didn't want to do any of the ordinary things that usually kept us busy, so I picked her up and we went to Neal's to sort through Judy's things from the hospital and put them away and to clean the house a bit. Mostly, we talked about Judy, her life continually running through our minds, like a video.

Neal took care of everything for the funeral. He planned the program to be sure it was special, like Judy. Judy didn't like anything that was ordinary—she liked the extraordinary, the unexpected. So Neal had the program designed with a dancer on the front and a signature from a letter written in her own handwriting: "Love, Judy."

On the evening of Judy's passing, Lori had asked each of the children to write down some thoughts about their mother. Tucker and Lyndsy wanted to read what they had written at the funeral, so Neal added their names to the program. Linda and I went with Neal to select the bouquet for the top of the casket. (He had picked out the only bronze, peach-lined casket the funeral home had.) As we started to get in the car, Derek came running out.

"Just a minute," Neal said, turning to pick him up. "I'll take him with me and then I'll know where he is."

"Already starting to think like a mother," Linda commented.

The flowers we decided on were peach talisman roses with white daisies and baby's breath.

On Friday morning when I awakened, I realized the viewing would be that night and the funeral the next day. Vaguely I wondered what I would wear. Clothes hadn't seemed important for a long time, but suddenly I was thinking about them. Linda and I had checked with Neal about the children's clothes, but I hadn't thought about me. I wanted to look special for Judy. I knew she would be there, and I wanted to look nice. I needed to erase the memory of the surgical clothes in which she had seen me for so long.

I made myself get out of bed and into a shower, said a prayer, and then went down to a dress shop near my home. Within thirty minutes—a record time—I tried on two dresses, both of which fit: a red dress with an unusual waist feature and a peach-colored silk one, trimmed with lace. I said another prayer of thanks and hurried home.

While I organized things at home, Vicki was with Neal. He had asked her, his mother, and Judy's hair sytlist—her cousin Sandy, who did her hair and was close to her—to go with him to the mortuary. Vicki told me about the experience later. It was the sweetest tribute a husband could pay to his beloved wife. He wanted to dress her himself to make sure everything was all right. The makeup would be the most difficult; her skin had taken on a dark cast because of the side effects of her illness.

There in the mortuary, Neal touched Judy's tiny feet, her toes pointed in like a dancer. He touched her small hands and talked about how beautiful she was. He was thoughtful, looking at her as if he didn't ever want to stop. He touched her head before fitting the wig. "I don't know if I want to cover it up," he said with a smile. "Most people wouldn't look good with a bald head, and Judy had beautiful hair, but her head is such a cute shape."

Later, when the makeup was complete, he said quietly, "I wish I had the power the Savior had. He raised Lazarus from the dead after four days. Judy hasn't been gone quite three days."

I had never known anyone who had helped lay out and dress the body of a loved one except my mother, who had done this for my baby sister who had died. But we lived in a small town that had no mortuaries. I remembered how tenderly she had talked about it.

Hundreds of people came to the viewing that Friday night. They were lined up when Milt and I arrived. All evening the line was long—people whom we hadn't seen for years.

As I stood there talking to people, in my head rang the words of a friend who had called me on the phone long distance. He and Judy had been good friends for a lot of years. His words on the phone still rang in my ears: "A valiant lady, a very valiant lady. She lived her life dynamically and left it the same way."

"Thank you," I said.

"She was blessed, Shirl," he went on. "The disease she had was a killer that shows no mercy."

How wonderful it was to have friends! I was busy all evening, greeting, talking, explaining, giving sympathy to those who had come to pay tribute to Judy and Neal and the children and to us, Judy's family. Some people we hadn't seen since Judy was a little girl, but they remembered her vibrant spirit, even as a child.

It was a long night. Devro was there, looking pale and needing to sit down sometimes. Lori stayed close by him. We were all there, even Loni and Blaine, who arrived in the middle of the evening. I didn't see them enter but suddenly felt Loni's arms around me. I knew I had subconsciously been waiting for something and wasn't sure just what until I felt her warmth and heard her cheerful, Judy-like voice. Blaine was right behind her. I was so grateful to see him. I ran to meet him and felt a wave of strength from his quiet, calm personality as he, too, put his arms around me.

I had never felt the family so close. Linda was there with her children—the twins giving strength to Judy's daughter Lyndsy; and Dale, Linda's husband, was taking care of details no one else thought about, as he always did. Vicki and Richard had brought their boys to be with Tucker and Spencer. Richard, who was the first of my daughter's husbands to join the family, had always been close to Judy.

All my sisters and brothers, some of them traveling long distances, were there with their children. The family seemed endless and their support eternal.

Milt stood up pretty well, with a lot of his friends there to support him. His brother and some other family members had arrived by plane, and that helped a lot. His sister, in a wheelchair, had made the long trip from Logan despite her own illness, and his mother, ninety-four years old, had sent word she would be at the funeral in the morning.

Family, friends, church leaders, and Judy lent us strength to carry us through that evening. Oh, yes, Judy was there. We all felt her influence. It was a happy feeling—like Judy.

It was as if she were trying to tell us that at last she was healed, she was free of the harnessing of a tired body and the worry that, after all she had been through, her cancer might return again. It was Judy's night, and her spirit radiated everywhere.

The children held up well too; young as they were, they took everything with dignity. Tucker said he had never been hugged by so many pretty girls. With their cousins beside them, Judy's children kept the evening lively.

Another group that touched my heart as they came through the line were Judy's dance students. She had given a lot of herself to her dancers, and they responded. They had waited for her to come back from the hospital and teach them again. Now that they knew she was gone, their hopes were shattered.

As the line finally came to an end, Neal asked me to remain and help him with finishing touches on Judy's dress for the funeral the next day. Milt and I stayed with Vicki and Richard and Sandy. While we worked, Neal talked about the program for the funeral and how he felt Judy had communicated to him through the spirit to let him know what she wanted. Then he made a request.

"I wanted to talk tomorrow," he said. "Devro spoke at his wife's funeral and I've always admired him for that, but I may not be physically up to that test. Shirl, if I can't and if I write a few things down, will you do it for me?"

Looking at him, I felt my throat tighten, but I answered without even thinking, "I'll do anything you ask me to do, Neal. Or at least I'll try."

This was one funeral where I thought I wouldn't have to sing or do anything but be there. I remembered singing at my father's funeral because it was his request, but for this one I hadn't planned on doing anything but attending, just being with the children and Neal. But after all Neal had done, I would not refuse anything he felt he needed to have me do. Neal was my son, as Judy was my daughter, and had been ever since their marriage.

CHAPTER 14

All night long, words ran through my mind, words I might say if Neal couldn't speak and asked me to do so. I wasn't used to reading other people's words and that worried me, so I thought of what needed to be said and what Judy might have me say. I had no idea what Neal had in mind, and there wouldn't be time to prepare except through praying. I did a lot of that, and finally my mind settled into sleep.

The next morning, Saturday, September 13, was a beautiful day. As the sun came through my windows, I pushed myself out of bed, showered, and put on my new peach-colored dress.

As Milt and I drove to Neal's home, the sunshine stayed with us. All signs of the torrential wind and rain storms we had had during Judy's last week in the hospital were gone. It was as if heaven were smiling.

As I walked into the house and made my way through rooms filled with flowers, Neal met me in the hall.

"Shirl," he said, smiling, "a new peach dress, Judy's color."

The look on his face showed he was pleased. "Shirl, I have a letter from Judy for you to read."

"A letter from Judy?"

"That's right. She came to see me last night. She wanted to say good-bye to everyone and spiritually dictated this letter to me. I've got it all ready for you."

I followed him to his office and he handed me a handwritten paper. As I read it, all the thoughts I had had through the night were put together in letter form. The letter covered every subject I'd been thinking about, but organized the ideas better than I had mentally organized them. Neal was right. It was from Judy. It sounded like Judy, sounded like what she would want to say.

As we entered the ward, where Judy's body, dressed in white temple robes, was lying peacefully, I was determined that we shouldn't have the long waiting lines of the night before. We decided to mill around among the people and talk to those we knew, leaving only Neal and the children standing beside the coffin. This worked out well, even though there were still many people there.

After the viewing, the family gathered around the casket while Devro gave the family prayer, his voice clear and his words full of love. Each of Judy's children had something special for their mother, to put in her casket. Tucker gave her a special musical recording he had made; Maren, a pair of her dancing slippers; Spencer, a bag of black licorice, which she loved; Lyndsy, a sealskin doll, "Ookpeek," the first doll Neal had given Judy after their marriage; and Derek, a black toy Porsche because Judy had always wanted a Porsche and had been saving for one. The children kissed their mother as they gave her the presents, and then Neal tied the bow on her veil and the casket was closed.

As we filed through the crowded chapel, I took my place on the front row with Milt's mother and the children.

The bishop conducted the service. It was not a sad funeral. It was more like the beginning of a new life than the end of an old one. For the family, it revealed a side of Judy that, outside the family circle, she had shared with others, a life full of friends as dear as brothers and sisters. And for her friends, it revealed the Judy we had known and loved so dearly.

Neal's sisters sang the opening song, "The Test," which tells of this life as a test for us all. Then Dale, who had helped so willingly and sympathetically through all the long months of Judy's illness, gave the opening prayer.

For the family tribute, Vicki had put together thoughts that explained Judy in a way only a loving sister could do. Vicki had been ill the night before and had been extremely pale after the viewing. Knowing that she needed special strength, that Judy would expect it of her, she had asked Richard to give her a blessing. Now, as she took the stand, her face was radiant, and there was no sign of the tears that had racked her body so often since Judy's illness was diagnosed.

"As an only child, I could hardly wait for my little sister to be born," she began. "She was fair, chubby, red-headed, and full of spunk. When I tried to hold her, she would fight to be released, probably because being only four, I didn't give Judy a feeling of security in my arms. But as she grew, I got my wish and Judy became my friend—a companion to enjoy everything with. She tagged after me those first few years. We had twin dresses, twin cowboy outfits, twin dolls for Christmas, and twin Easter dresses."

Vicki went on to tell several stories from their childhood, illustrating Judy's creativity, independence, and standards of excellence. She delivered her message beautifully, ending with this tribute:

"The most important people in Judy's life were Neal, the children, her family, and Heavenly Father. Though she did not want to leave and fought courageously to stay, she knew her children would be well taken care of; she knew Neal would rise to the challenge because that's the way he is.

"The night before Judy died, I told her how much we loved her and how proud we were of her courage. She smiled and her reaction was to express gratitude for Devro and Lori, who gave so much to help her. It pleased Devro to be her transplant donor, and after she died he said, 'Sore hips never felt so good. We gave it our best.'

"Judy is not really dead, only out of pain and suffering. She is still our sister, friend, mother, aunt, daughter, and Neal's wife. She will, you can be assured, be doing her usual good deeds for us all where she is now, and we can continue to do many needed things for her family. Tucker, Maren, Spencer, Lyndsy, and Derek: do well in school, develop your talents, clean your rooms, be thoughtful of each other. That's what she expects."

Next on the program was Tucker, who read the tribute he had started to write the night Judy died:

"My mom was a great person. I'll remember lots of things about her. She helped me. I hated playing the piano, but Mom thought I needed to learn how to play. She spent hours practicing with me. This was really hard because she didn't even know how to read music. Then there's school work. When I had a report to do, she stayed up really late with me working on it. She would look up stuff in the encyclopedia and tell me what to write.

"For birthdays and Christmas, we really knew what to get her: jewelry! I think she had more jewelry than 'Mr. T.' She took me all sorts of places: football, soccer games, car pooling, and shopping. My mom loved sports. You could say she was a 'jock.' She watched while I tried for hours to get up on my ski. Nothing seemed to work, not even getting up on two skis and dropping one. But I finally did it. She was so proud of my improvement that for graduation from Hillside, she bought me my own ski.

"Because Mom was so good at sports, she was also very competitive. She did not like to lose at games. She wanted to be the best at water-skiing. I'm still in a race with her. However, there is one competition she lost. When I was eleven years old, I became taller than she was!

"My mom was a strong person. She fought her disease and the painful chemotherapy. She had courage. She had many friends, as I found out last night for three hours, standing in a line, having only Certs and water to eat. I'm going to miss her a lot . . . all of us will. She was a great mom, and there will never be anyone else like her."

Before he sat down, Tucker announced that Lyndsy had something to say. He hadn't faltered. He was the true son of an actress who knew the show must go on.

Lyndsy got up to speak next. She read an original poem titled, "Special Things I Remember About Mom."

I love to go shopping with my Mom.
My Mom has pretty eyes.
I like my Mom's pretty red hair.
My Mom has pretty nails.
Sometimes I feel her inside me.
She helps me read my books.
I know my Mom loves me.
She taught me to dance.
She taught me to talk, play, and to sing.
At Christmas time I am the only person who gets
a stuffed toy.
My Mom always takes me Christmas shopping.
She wears pretty earrings
and pretty necklaces and pretty makeup
and she wears pretty hairdos.
I get good books from her.
I like the toys that she gives me.
She is the best Mom I ever had.
She bought pretty clothes for me, and pretty shoes and
pretty dolls
and good candy and coloring books.
She took good pictures of me.
And, it was fun buying clothes and buying things for
school,
and going skiing at Bear Lake.
And she wanted to see the cabin.

As Lyndsy left the pulpit and took her place with the family, I thought about Judy and the cabin at Bear Lake. She was so determined to have it ready for the children in the summer. We received word from the workers at Bear Lake that the roof went on the cabin the day she died. I couldn't help thinking how the children's talks presented a mother image every woman dreams of creating for her children—a pattern, a guideline of what a mother can be in the lives of her children.

The second musical number, sung by the Maxfield sisters, was one of Judy's songs from Peter Pan, "I Won't Grow Up." The song was not only a sweet memory of the past but also symbolic of Judy's life. Why hadn't I realized that before?

Several of Judy's many friends gave short tributes. They all talked about the things they had learned from Judy. Summing them up, short of individual experiences, one phrase rang in my mind: *"She taught me how to live and she taught me how to die."* Those words seemed to echo the thoughts of all who knew her.

Then it was my turn. Neal had asked that all the cousins stand to one side of the pulpit while I talked, so they would be in place to sing the last song afterwards. As they assembled and I made my way to the stand, I was talking to Judy in my heart. This was her message; I wanted to read it as she would have me do it. It was "A Letter from Judy":

Dear friends and family:

I want to thank each of you for your faith and prayers in my behalf. You have helped me get through the toughest challenge of my life. I have felt your love, and want you to know that my heart is full of love for each of you.

These past nine and a half months have been full of pain and uncertainty. But they have also been some of the best months of my life. I have had time to reflect on my relationship with my Heavenly Father and know that he loves me and would not want me to suffer without purpose. I know that he would not take me from my family without a special reason. I have faith and trust in his wisdom and am willing to comply to his will.

I am grateful for the time I have had to prepare my family for my absence. I have also been given time to spend with my relatives and close friends, and to share with you the love in my heart for all you have done to make my life happy and complete. Each of you has strengthened me and made it easier to go through the treatments I have been given.

I want you to know that I was given the best of medical care. The nurses were so kind and attentive and the doctors prescribed for me the correct medications. It was the will of Heavenly Father for them to cure me twice and give me time to complete the last details of my life, but be ineffective the third time to make me well.

Thanks to Devro, who successfully gave me his bone marrow and platelets. And to my angel mother, Shirley, who came to the hospital this week and said she wasn't leaving until I got well—thanks, I am well. I am free from pain for the first time since I was a young child with Perthes' disease. I can run, and jump, and dance, and have full rotation of my hips. And I will never again know the pains of mortal life.

I want my children to know that I love each of you very much. I will be there to help you from time to time. Do your best in everything you do, and stay close to your Heavenly Father. You must be stronger now that I am gone, but I will be more help to you from here.

I want Neal to know that I love him and will miss him, and I am grateful for the past eighteen exciting years of marriage we have had. Heavenly Father has timed my hospital stays so that we could attend the candy conventions together in February and July, and have extra trips, too. He helped us spend more time together than at any other period of our marriage. These pleasant memories will sustain you until we embrace in the spirit world many years from now. I will come and escort you as others have come to escort me.

Thanks, again, to each of you. Life is eternal, and we will meet again and renew the love we share today. I look forward to that day.

Love, Judy

I walked off the stand, and the children and cousins assembled sang a medley of songs, including "Families Can Be Together Forever" and "I Am a Child of God."

Vicki's husband, Richard, who was almost a second father to Derek, offered the benediction. We were all joined together—in-laws were not in-laws now, but brothers and sisters—and Richard's prayer confirmed the depth of his and our feelings.

As we filed out the side door of the chapel reverently and quietly, there seemed to be a general uplifting of spirits. At the cemetery, a beautiful display of flowers was arranged beside Judy's grave. Milton gave the prayer dedicating the site. He was so broken up that I don't know how he did it, but he did a beautiful job. His Judy was gone, and he blessed the place where her body would rest until the morning of her resurrection.

It was a friendly scene, people loving each other and basking in the sun of that beautiful day, basking in the goodness that had been expressed. A cousin offered to dry some flowers for Judy's children and Neal, so, with Neal's permission, I plucked some of the roses from the bouquet blanketing her casket. Others came forward also to get a flower of remembrance. And the children chose flowers for bouquets to be put in their rooms at home. Afterwards, we returned to the ward, where food was served under the direction of the ward Relief Society.

Then it was time to go home. We had done all we could for the present. Judy was at rest, and the details had been taken care of. I felt high-strung, the way I had sometimes felt when talking to Judy, driving forward on the strength of newly acquired inner energy and knowledge, mixed with heartfelt gratitude that my prayers had been answered, that Judy hadn't lingered to suffer while her mortal body deteriorated further before our eyes. I would not take anything away from her earned glory and goodness with my own self-pity, not now, not on this day that belonged to Judy.

I knew there would be days ahead when I could relax enough to cry and when I would hurt for Neal and the children, and I knew I would do all I could to help fill their void. There would be days ahead when I would miss her terribly. But no matter how much I missed her now or in the days to come, I knew it wouldn't be as bad as waking up in the morning and knowing she was in the hospital frightened and fighting for her life.

I was aware there would be times to come when I would envy her victory over this mortal existence, envy the fact that her work here was finished. There would be times when I would be angry that she had gone first and that I had not been allowed the natural joy of a mother to be there to greet her when she came. There would be days when I would grieve and search for her, and days when I would remember the misery of her suffering in obedience to laws she didn't fully understand.

A feeling of great pride filled my heart, a feeling that surpassed every mortal emptiness and reached into a realm of newness, as if I had been allowed a quick look into the beginning of eternity.

Yes, for Judy, it was graduation day! All of her befores were over. She had earned her land of beauty and excellence, had received her degree of glory step by step as she made daily decisions, and had gone on to a place of higher learning, into a new dimension of preparation where our lives would all come together again someday. Judy had stepped through the veil of this mortal existence into the beginning of forever.

EPILOGUE

In a quiet cemetery not far from our home is a headstone, cut from peach-colored granite, with a sculpture of a pretty girl drawn by her husband and chiseled in the center of the stone. The birth and death of Judy Lyn Sealy are registered there. On one corner is a sculptured water ski. On another is an enlarged copy of the ring with which Neil won Judy. On the third corner are indented forms of candies. And on the fourth is Judy's logo of a lovely dancer.

ACKNOWLEDGMENTS

My thanks and appreciation to the following:

Judy, for the life she led.

Judy's husband, Neal Maxfield, and their children, Tucker, Maren, Spencer, Lyndsy, and Derek—for all they have done, for all they are, and for all they are becoming.

All the Maxfields—Neal's parents, brothers and sisters, and their families—who loved Judy like their own.

Judy's sisters and their husbands—Vicki and Richard Clayton, Linda and Dale Ottley, and Loni and Blaine Hatch—and especially Judy's brother, Devro, and his wife, Lori, who came so far and did so much.

My husband, Milton, for always being there for all of us.

All who helped during Judy's illness and afterwards—those who brought gifts and food and did small and big favors to show their love for Judy and her family.

Gene and Marna Cook, special friends who helped and cared.

Those who read the manuscript and offered helpful suggestions.

All who allowed their names to be used in this story of our Judy.

And the many, many people whose floral offerings built the beautiful setting for Judy's last production.